Lifetime Rules I Learned from My Seat on the Bench

A Game Plan for Life for the Student-Athlete

Edward Yergalonis

Expecting Excellence Press—Cranford, NJ
ISBN: 979-8-9876131-2-2
eBook ISBN: 979-8-9876131-3-9
Library of Congress Control Number:
Title: *Lifetime Rules I Learned from My Seat on the Bench: A Game Plan for Life for the Student-Athlete*
Author: Edward Yergalonis
Digital distribution | 2023
Paperback | 2023

Dedication

This book is dedicated to the student athletes who give their all each week for their school, community, parents, coaches, and themselves. Always remember that your success will be determined by your positive attitude and how hard you work.

Why I wrote this book and why you should read it.

Time flies! Believe it. Your playing career ends quickly. Your work career flies by. One day you are worrying about a salary increase to help make ends meet and the next day you are planning your retirement. I can say the same about having a family. One day you are bottle feeding your daughter and the next day you are walking her down the wedding aisle. It is just life. That is how it works. There are many twists and turns and many difficulties along the way. Yes, there are good times and bad times. You cannot change that, but what you can do is to make informed choices along your journey.

Your choices are all ahead of you. Make informed choices. Use my experiences to help shape your own experiences. And yes, they will be your experiences, yours alone. Thcy will not be your parent's choices nor will they be your coach's choices. Listen to them and process their information as you make your own choices and set the course for your own life. Your parents, coaches or friends cannot live your life. This life is all yours. Make the most of it and be able to look back on it and be happy with your choices.

You will pass through many phases of your life. These phases will all look and seem different to you. One can compare life to a game. You have phases in a game and you have phases in your life. Momentum changes throughout the contest. Momentum changes in life.

In a game, each of your decisions and actions will have consequences. And these consequences vary in importance depending on what part of the game you are in. The same is true for life. For example, if you fumble or miss a block or tackle in the first quarter, the team can overcome the result of your mistake. However, if you miss that same block or tackle or fumble the ball on the goal line with the scored tied and thirty seconds to go in the game, the team may never recover. Your actions and decisions vary in importance based on the situation. This is true throughout life. Think long and hard about lifetime choices. When necessary, call a time out and use that timeout to regroup or break some negative momentum. Choose wisely.

As that Monday morning quarterback, I am undefeated. I make a great after-dinner speaker telling you about all my "should haves" and "could haves." However, I wish I had some benefits of my experience before I had to make some of my lifetime choices. Don't we all wish for that do-over in life? In a friendly game of golf, this do- over is called a "Mulligan." I think most people want that "Mulligan" in life. You know, that drive you make in golf where your ball ends up on the adjacent fairway. And you knew your swing was off the minute you pulled the club back. Most times, that second drive is better. Did you ever really think about why that second shot is better? It is simple. You learned from that first drive and probably made some change to your swing. The same is true in life. People want that "Mulligan" in his or her life to make some corrections. Unfortunately, when the golf games really count, there is no such thing as a "Mulligan." The same is also for life.

No one wants to sit on the bench. You are on a team to compete and play. That is a given. And if you are a gifted athlete, you probably rarely, if ever, sat on the bench. The minute you learned to play any competitive sport; you were probably the best.

People saw your advanced skill, even in the kindergarten youth soccer league. Everyone knows it and you know it. Your community's high school soccer coach would watch those Saturday morning games picking out his or her varsity team for ten years down the road. The private coaching lessons and travel teams would soon start for you. And then one day, the coach forces you to sit on the bench and watch because suddenly he or she deems you are just not good enough. It is mentally devastating and exhausting. It is like waking up from a bad dream. I know this because I lived it.

As you transition from high school to college, prepare yourself to spend some time on that bench. Very few athletes can graduate from high school and immediately contribute to an NCAA athletic program in the upcoming fall. Will you be this immediate contributor? I hate to burst your bubble, but it will probably not be you. The odds are just against you. Do not get tricked by watching television and seeing that freshman star quarterback slice up the opposing defense. Take my word for it. That guy is the exception to the rule.

Programs often red shirt freshmen to preserve eligibility. During this year, they expect you to get bigger and stronger and, of course, smarter. You need to learn the system without the pressure of competing. When you are being recruited, ask about your prospective team's red shirting practice. Ask the older players about this because I believe they will tell you the truth. For me, I languished for four years on the bench, seeing only sporadic action as a backup player. Pay close attention to my story because you can learn from it.

I was a pretty good high school football player and football will be the backdrop of my tales. Please substitute any sport that you wish for because the parallels will be similar if not right on the money. Making the leap from high school to college athletics is a gigantic leap.

The game, especially the mental processes, just moves at a much quicker rate. For me, the mental game was much harder to adjust to. In high school, I never had to think and react at that rate of speed.

I hope that as you prepare to leave high school, your number one goal must be to get a college degree. Period! End of discussion. Frame all your pursuits and choices with that in mind. Find the best situation that seems right for you to get that degree. Because very few of you will have the chance to play at the professional level. And if you play at the next level, your career will be short.

You must prepare for life. Even though you now may be that five-star recruit, there will be life after football. And if you are lucky enough to play at the next level, very few players leave the professional game set financially for life. And keep in mind that there is only a finite need for sportscasters, so yes, the lessons in this book will apply to you.

Even if you are a NIL (Name, Image, and

Likeness) athlete with exceptional skills, there are still valuable lessons embedded in this book.

For others that read this book, you can take my lessons to your workplace. I have found that the lessons that I will talk about translate easily to any business or workplace. Any recent college graduate will benefit from internalizing my rules and applying them to a new job. I am convinced that if you know my commandments, you will spend less time on the bench, either with your team or in your new corporate environment.

My colleagues will quickly share that I think and write using athletic analogies and metaphors. If that annoys you, this book is probably not for you. But if you personalize my rules, you will be able to apply my commandments anywhere.

In business, when I write about spending time on the bench, think of that in terms of spending your career in an entry level position. Or perhaps, spending two or three years with a company and at the end of that time period, you are just let go.

You may spend your entire professional life bouncing between entry-level jobs. But if you possess a competitive spirit and drive, your genetic make-up will not support this. If you are stuck in this rut, going nowhere, having no real "playing time," (seeing important work action), it will drive you insane. If you let my rules guide you, I can see a bright future on your horizon.

If within your DNA you possess a competitive drive, sitting on the bench, either literally or figuratively, will mentally torture you. I am sure of that. I lived it.

Pre-game planning

*S*ome things to think about:

- *Know who you are. Life can be confusing. Stay in your lane and never take on more than you can handle.*
- *When you are starting an unfamiliar experience, keep your eyes and ears wide open and your mouth shut.*
- *You have a long career ahead of you. Take your time and slow down. Always remember that patience is a virtue.*
- *Stay focused on your prize. Use your laser-like focus to attain both your short term and long-term goals. For the college student-athlete, your prize is your college degree. Never forget that!*
- *Check your ego at the door.*
- *Learning is a lifelong process. Learning is never terminal. Use every opportunity to learn from others.*
- *Work to become comfortable in your own skin. Remember that you are who you are. Use your strengths to your advantage.*

Know Thyself.

My life story would probably bore you to death, so let's agree that I always felt that I was born with a football or baseball in my hand. I can remember playing in the streets or in someone's backyard. I can recall playing a game of football with two other guys, and one of us would be the steady quarterback. Sadly, I do not see that kind of play from our young people today. You do not need some organized youth league to learn the game or hone your skills. You do not need this youth league to nurture your love of the game.

Thankfully, I always weighed too much to play youth league or "Pop Warner" football. I can recall horror stories of some of my friends at eleven years of age donning rubber suits to cut weight to make the team. I hope and pray that this ridiculous and dangerous practice is a thing of the past. Initially, I was mad at my parents, but now I am thankful they did not let me try, because after 8 years of football, I was exhausted. I was physically and mentally spent.

I had a stellar high school career where I achieved some success. I was "All This" and "All That" and thought it assured me of playing in the NFL. Being an offensive lineman, you rarely received any public accolades. You played the position because you had the skill set and size to play it. Perhaps you just might have been the biggest kid in the school.

On the first day, you thought you would be a great fullback, but after practice, they moved you to the offensive line. It is almost like a banishment when your running back or receiver bubble breaks. Never forget that you are who you are. That might be your first lesson you will learn from this book. You need to stay in your lane and contribute to your team's success. I knew I would never touch the football. I had to get over that and learn to contribute to the success of the team in any manner.

You learn quickly that the team comes before your individual wants or needs. I had to check my ego at the door. Maybe offensive linemen learn this lesson the quickest of all football players. Will you be able to do the same? Believe it or not, some people can never do this and his or her career will reflect that deficiency.

If you are a recruited quarterback, always remember you could switch to defense or wide receiver. And yes, I know a quarterback or two that was moved to tight end. Your new teammates will tease you in good nature. Can you deal with that? Maybe you can and maybe you cannot. But you need to think about it because it can happen.

Colleges recruit elite athletes and most quarterbacks fit that bill. And unlike other positions on the team, only one quarterback can play at a time.

I ended up being a recruited scholarship athlete and attended the College of William and Mary in Virginia. The entire recruiting process was a whirlwind. Enjoy it because once it is over, things change. Relationships change. It was a sad revelation that the coach that recruited me barely spoke to me when I arrived on campus. He was not my position coach, but I somehow felt that in this way he let me down.

And yes, your head will grow and you will love being the center of attention in your recruiting world. During the season, you will get up early in the morning to run for the newspaper to see how the papers and social media tell your story from the night before.

For me, I thought William and Mary provided the perfect place to combine my athletic ability and interests with a fine education. On my visits there, I felt comfortable. I felt I fit in. I felt I could go there and continue my path to stardom. Unfortunately, it did not take long for my personal bubble to burst.

I graduated in four years and had a decent academic record. My athletic career was marginal. I became a teacher and a coach. They promoted me to various positions, including curriculum supervisor, high school vice principal, middle school principal, and high school principal. After serving as an assistant superintendent for some years, I retired from my position as superintendent of schools. I made it to the top of my career ladder and it had nothing to do with my athletic ability. But I knew how to be part of a team which is a critical skill to hone for life.

I also knew that I did not have to be the star of that team. During my career, I had the privilege of working with thousands of wonderful students and hundreds, if not thousands, of wonderful adults. Choosing education as a career path enabled me to stay close to the game, and I loved working with young student-athletes. And I could do all of this in my hometown. I could return home and give back to the community that gave so much to me. My football team won a state championship while I was the head football coach. That 1984 team was a great one and was the last team to win a state championship from my school. Can you imagine that?

Some people may also believe that it is easy to repeat as a champion. Let me assure you, it is not. One must never forget that to win a championship, every break must go your way. Every bounce of the ball must go your way and every close officiating call must be yours. As a champion, you now also have a target on your back. Real champions get used to that.

There were not any superstars on that team. It was just a group of young athletes who worked hard and always kept a great attitude. Some might say I led a storybook life.

Through my work as an educator, I could open many educational doors for my students. I cherished my work with the College Board and the Advanced Placement Program. Those programs helped facilitate tremendous academic success for my urban students.

I forged a great relationship with Dr. P. Roy Vagelos, the former chairperson of the Board of Merck and Co., and great humanitarian. I was most proud of my work with Dr. Vagelos as we facilitated some of my students going on to the best universities in the world. It was hard to dream about this kind of success until we forged our relationship. I fondly sit back and look at the picture on my wall of my five medical doctors that we helped produce. I still cherish my relationship with these scholars today, just like I cherish my relationship with my former players.

But the question that keeps nagging at me is "Was it all worth it?" Was the scholarship worth it? It was nice that this scholarship provided me with four years of tuition, room, board, books, and laundry money. William and Mary provided everything for me. I knew my parents were proud and happy. But what did I give up and sacrifice personally for this scholarship?

Yes, wait until the end of this story to see my answer to that question. You might find my response to that question surprising, so wait until the end. I have chased this answer in my head for many years. And I think I finally have this answer. Sit back and relax and as you digest my rules, try to apply them to your life. Take my rules and make them your rules and I hope that you have the same success in life that I had.

Commandments I Learned from My Seat on the Bench

- *Do you want to be the small fish in that big pond or be the big fish in a small pond? This is a genuine dilemma. You must also know the job market and your competition.*

- *Your athletic scholarship is your job. Do not kid yourself. Once you sign on that dotted line, they own you.*

- *It is all about effort and attitude. Never forget that.*

- *Every team and every organization have internal politics. You must learn how the system works and learn how to live in this environment.*

- *Keep your ego in check.*

- *You are never as good or as bad as you might think. You are never as good as your parents think. Be humble.*

- *You are finally on your own. Home is in your rearview mirror. Being in love is grand, but....*
- *Know how to take feedback like a champ.*

- *There is a mental aspect to everything. At each step along the way, the system plays faster, both physically and mentally. You must learn how to advocate for yourself. Academics are important!*

- *The player / coach or the employer /employee relationship is a delicate balance. Know when to pull the plug and move on.*

Tip Sheet #1

Your first dilemma is finding the answer to this question. Do you want to be that small fish in a big pond or that big fish in a small pond?

Some things to think about:

- *Your chances of playing any sport professionally are slim.*
- *In any pond, there is only room for so many fish.*
- *Everyone likes to dream big. Live in the present and live in*
- *reality.*
- *At your position, is the deck stacked against you?*
- *It is important to fit in. Does your team look and act like you? What about others on campus? How do they feel about scholarship athletes?*
- *Know what makes you happy.*

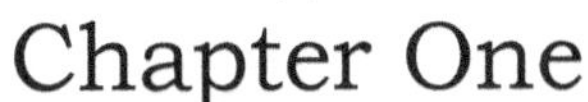

Chapter One

I cannot answer that opening question for you. However, I can ask you to think about it. Some people will attempt to answer that question by believing that they can be that big fish in that big pond. Good luck.

In many situations, just like that lead sled dog, there probably is room for only one lead dog on your team. Will that be you? And while you reflect on that question, I admonish you to answer it honestly. However, I believe that ultimately there can only be one lead fish in a pond that contains so many other big fish. Please do not forget that, depending upon the pond, size is all relative.

Let us get this straight right up front. You are probably not going to play in the NFL or the NBA. The odds are clearly against you. You may feel that you are the one that is going to beat those odds. Experts agree that the chances of getting struck by lightning are like those of playing in the NBA or NFL. Lightning strikes are rare. Playing in a professional league is just as rare. You get my point.

Let's look at it another way. How many people enter the casino looking to become rich? Stand outside of the casino and you can watch people trekking home broke. Maybe they just lost the rent money or the grocery money. The odds are clear and with the house. That is how casinos make money. Casinos know that in the long run, they are going to come out on top. It is next to impossible to beat the house.

Be mentally prepared to face the reality that beating the gambling house or the "professional athletic house" is a tough challenge. Of course, "shoot for the stars," but understand your chances of catching that star. Let us just say it is very unlikely for you to beat the "house."

Okay, let us assume you are one of the lucky ones and make into the NFL. Understand that the average career length of an NFL player is 3.3 years. If you are a running back, that career average dips to 2.5 years. If your goal is the NBA, then your career lasts about 4.5 years. And please do not forget that most do not see the big money until the second contract. Likely, you will probably look for a new career at 27. In that short time period, it is a fact, you will have to work again. Very few athletes can live for a lifetime on the money he or she earned as a professional in this short time period.

Now, let us go down that road of injuries.

If you are that lucky to have been a professional, it will have taken its toll on your body. That is a given. Now you need to think about your second career with all the aches and pains received in professional sports. Residual effects from injuries can last a lifetime.

I chose The College of William and Mary and William and Mary chose me (And I am sure that during my four years there both W&M and I thought we made an awful choice.) It checked all my boxes. I thought it was the right size pond for me.

Before you laugh at William and Mary, because many people will, understand in my era, our football schedule over my four-year career included schools such as Virginia, Virginia Tech, Wake Forest, Mississippi State, Boston College, Rutgers, East Carolina, Navy, Pittsburgh, Louisville, and our regular conference opponents Richmond, VMI, Furman, The Citadel and Delaware. And believe it or not, we were competitive in most of the games, beating several of the big boys.

Today, William and Mary football is regularly competing for the national championship at the FCS level.

Academically, it is hard to beat the excellence found at William and Mary. William and Mary often receives national recognition for its academic excellence, and it is ranked within the top 30 universities, particularly among public universities.

I believe that William and Mary is the perfect place to blend both academic and athletic excellence.

Before committing, find out how many scholarship athletes play your position. That may give you a good sign of your playing possibilities. In my year, I was one of about seven or eight offensive linemen brought in to campus. I never asked that question, but I expected to help rebuild the offensive line at W & M. Just by looking at these numbers may have given me a sign of my playing prospects. My competition for playing time immediately and in the future was going to be intense.

And when I stood in the room for the first time with my offensive linemen, I was one of the smallest. It was a hard adjustment, going from the physically biggest man on my high school campus to now being one of the smallest in my position room. If I was told this, I probably would not have cared, because I thought I was going to be that one to beat all the odds. I found out over my career that recruited athletes have an inflated opinion of themselves.

During the recruiting period, try to evaluate if you fit into the culture of your chosen school. For example, if you are a northern city person, are you going to be comfortable going to a rural school in the deep south? Likewise, if you come from a southern school with warmer climates, are you going to adjust to the bitter cold of that small midwestern town? If you come from the city, are you going to adjust to the school that is in the middle of nowhere?

I can recall when I arrived in Williamsburg, Virginia, for my college days, there was not even a McDonald's in town. If my memory serves me correctly, the first McDonald's restaurant arrived during my junior year. At home, there was a different fast-food restaurant on every corner. This tale is not about McDonalds, it is about culture.

Likewise, do people in your academic community look and act like you? And if they don't, are you going to be comfortable there? These are all important items to consider before signing on the dotted line. I never thought of those things. I wish I did.

By now, you can see where the tip sheet is heading. I was in a bit over my head athletically, even in that small pond. Of course, this surprised me. Many of the big boys recruited me. What if I had chosen a much bigger pond? I would have been more out of my league. Also, I was in a bit over my head academically. Although I had very good SAT scores and was a 4.0 student, I was in over my head academically. I had to work extremely hard in the classroom to keep my head above water. On road trips, most of us brought our books and read and studied on the plane or bus.

I brag to my grown kids about my William and Mary degree. My youngest daughter usually reminds me I likely would not have gotten in to W&M if not for football. She is probably right. Most schools have some wiggle room academically with recruited scholarship athletes. But I am proud to say that I busted my butt academically and graduated in four years. And I am also proud to say that I never missed a football practice, team meeting or team work out.

Yet the nagging question persists, would I have been happier in a smaller pond?

What about you? What size pond are you prepared to swim in?

Tip Sheet #2

Playing college football is a job. Do not kid yourself. Once you sign on that dotted line, they own you.

Some things to think about:

- *Forget about all those head inflating conversations. This is a business, and you just signed off on it.*
- *Whose best interest is that college coach looking out for? Yours? His?*
- *The coach's job is to win, not babysit you.*
- *To get noticed, you must exceed expectations. First impressions are critical.*
- *Free time? Forget it. They will account for just about every second of your day.*
- *Everything becomes nothing more than a series of competitions. Are you up for that?*
- *Your dreams will never automatically just come true. You must earn everything.*

Chapter Two

After coming down from your recruiting high, reality sets in. You have chosen your college. Please do not feel bad because, for most college recruits, this is a simple, almost unnoticed process. Most recruits do not get that press conference where you can display your creative side and select that hat of your choice. Most recruits will not even have some sort of signing ceremony at your high school. It does not matter; it is time to start the next phase of your life.

For the past two to three years, you have had many adults telling you how great you are. You relished the attention. Although bothersome, you enjoyed all the social media contacts and phone calls with your recruiter. At school, you enjoyed getting called to the Guidance Office or your coach's office to meet with a college coach. Each one of them telling you how great you are and how their program needs you. They overwhelm your family when the head coach visits your home to make the pitch to your parents. Each coach assuring your parents that they will always be there to guide and support you. They assure your parents that they will take care of you, always looking out for your best interests. I like to believe in the sincerity of that coach. But understand this: their job is to win. Can you help them win? The way they treat you will change based on the answer to that question.

Let me digress a bit here because it is important that you know what I am about to tell you. To survive as a coach, you need to win. If you do not win, they will fire you. That is the life of a coach.

Also, the nature of an assistant coach's life is that you are getting fired or looking to move up to an improved opportunity. The college coach is probably looking at seven to ten moves in his or her coaching life. These moves often are sudden and unexpected. That is one reason it is essential that you pick the school and not the head coach or position coach. Assistant coaches get tied to that head coach and when he moves on, the assistant usually moves on. When a staff gets fired, everyone gets fired. Many times, this includes football secretaries and equipment managers. It hit me hard when my position coach left just prior to my senior season. I had to start over with a new coach and that coach was now looking out for his future, and I was not part of it. I get it now. I did not understand it then.

Now, suddenly, you arrive on campus to

start your season and the school year. That is right, the school year. Do not forget that you are supposed to be a student- athlete. It does not take you long to realize that something has changed.

I strongly recommend that you get on campus as soon as possible. Take advantage of any early high school graduation. Enroll early. Think about starting the next step in life by going to school early after graduating. This may give you the opportunity to get a jump on some classes, get to know your teammates and get started in your team's conditioning program. I can assure you that you will not be big or strong enough to compete for college playing time immediately. Most times, it will just take time and a lot of hard work. This is especially true for offensive linemen.

I arrived on campus terribly out of shape for my first season. I followed all the guidelines that the coaches sent me and I was feeling pretty good about myself. Boy, was I mistaken. All summer, I thought I was really "kicking butt" following the summer work out that they provided me, only to find out that I was clueless. Reflectively, I am not sure that I ever recovered from this conditioning set back.

You know by now that you never get a second chance to make a good first impression. I bombed that one. I am sure that my coaches probably believed that I was a recruiting mistake. Me? This "All County," all-star a recruiting mistake? Later, when I began my coaching career, I believe that I probably would have thought of myself in this same light.

I said earlier that your relationship quickly changes with your recruiting coach. I truly believed that this same guy who sat in my living room, kissing my butt, and schmoozing my parents, would somehow be there for me. Boy, was I wrong.

He was not my position coach, and he barely spoke to me. I do not think that he was a bad guy, but you never realize the intense pressure that a college coach is under. Was this the same guy that promised my parents that he would look out for me? Shoot, he did not even talk to me for God's sake. And I was struggling. I remain optimistic that things have changed in that regard and there are more support systems built in to help guys like me. And although I surely felt isolated and alone, I knew I was not the only one struggling. Maybe it was just part of the process. You know, growing up. And although you are clearly not alone in your struggles, you never would admit it to any of your teammates and friends. You just kept on plugging along.

One of the worst things you can do is to

bond with others somehow that are feeling as bad as yourself. Instead of serving as some sort of support group, it only reinforces your unhappiness and negativity. A lifetime lesson is to seek the positive and happy people and bond with them. As hard as that might be, it will be a life-changing action. You know that misery loves company. Disassociate yourself from those that are miserable.

Throughout the process, I never knew how to advocate for myself. Somewhere in the maturation process, I missed that class. When you learn how to advocate for yourself, I am optimistic that you will not hit rock bottom. You will know how to find the resources to help yourself. And perhaps sadly, to break this paradigm, you only must speak up. And of course, this is easier said than done.

I used the word intense earlier to describe my recruiting coach. I learned quickly that one big difference between college and high school athletics is the intensity of everything. Everything moves at a faster speed. Of course, people are bigger and stronger, but making the speed change is critical. I believe people can only hit you so hard. However, it is the speed with which they hit you that is the big change.

As an offensive lineman in high school, I dominated my block by positioning myself where my opponent was lined up and executing the block. However, in college, if you do that, you will never make a block because your person will be long gone. Technique and mechanics also became more important. In high school, one could actually "out big" a person. In college, using the wrong technique will paralyze you. If you do not believe me, just try it.

The program now owns you. Accept that. Your coaches will account for every second of your day. Get used to it. It is now a way of life. Every day you will be engaged in tasks like being on the field, attending meetings, watching films, going to classes, and conditioning or lifting weights. You will be told when to sleep and when to eat. Probably you will get up before the crack of dawn for either a practice or work out or to attend an early morning class. You will be told when you can go home and when you need to return.

Please do not expect to be getting home during the first semester, it just will not happen. And please do not believe that NCAA guidelines now in place about the time you may spend on team activities will help you. I believe that every successful program finds a legal way to circumvent these guidelines. Take my word for that. When you are not on the field, you will be in meeting rooms, meeting with your position coach or watching film.

I had a hard time making this change.

Yes, the change of being told what to do 24 hours a day, seven days a week. You have that scholarship, but in doing so, you signed away part of your freedom. I do not want to mislead you. Each year got better. No, they did not let up, you just got used to it. Your mindset changed. You are the one that must adjust and change. Your coaches and their expectations will not change for you. I was smart enough to make this change. Some were not, and they usually became academic causalities.

Programs were over-recruiting, leading to NCAA limits on scholarships. Scholarship limits have helped remedy this situation because coaches cannot succeed if they recruit too many scholarship mistakes. I never felt as though any coach was ever looking to run me off. If I kept up my end of the bargain, I never felt that my scholarship was going to be taken away. Do not forget that scholarships are for one year at a time. This topic is another good thing to talk about and learn about before you sign on the dotted line. Find out what will happen to your scholarship if your injury occurs away from the practice field. For example, what happens if you get into a car accident and injured where you cannot play football again? Find out what happens if you trip and fall down the stairs in your home and cannot play football again? Assume nothing!

Find out how many players leave yearly and determine if you can find out why they left the program. Transferring has become baffling now. It is hard to keep up with all the transfer rules right now. It is critical for you to understand the transfer portal and how that affects your position and playing time. For example, you have been a good team guy and have patiently waited your turn to be on the field. Then one day you wake up and find that the team just signed a stud, yes, a graduate transfer to take your prospective spot. The transfer portal has allowed teams to win quickly, but there is always a cost to pay and the one who pays it is the guy that has been waiting his turn to play. You have become collateral damage. (By the time you are reading this book, the transfer portal will probably look a great deal different from it today. It is your job to stay informed.)

If you are a scholarship player, you are used to being a starter. When the first team was called, you assumed your position. You probably did this for at least three years in high school. You never left the field. Just visualize going from getting all the first team reps to now running on the scout squad. It can be humiliating. My coaches at W&M called the offensive scout team "beavers" and the defensive scout team "meatballs," which made it even more humiliating for me. It was demeaning. For me, I now had to get the first team defense ready for the game. We ran the opponent's plays off cards held up in the huddle. Please understand that the coaches are only going to give those players meaningful reps who are going to play in the weekly game. To make matters worse, I had to practice daily against the first team defensive tackle whose first move was to grab the fat on the side of my ribs with each hand, stand me up and twist. It was excruciating. In the locker room, after practicing my fellow "beavers," and I would compare the black and blue marks left by this guy. He was a great guy, and an excellent player. He was only practicing his game technique.

What is the key? INTENSITY! You cannot practice with the same level of intensity that you did in high school because if you do, you will never see the field. Successful teams make every play a competition where each player in each individual battle must get better on every play. It is both mentally and physically intense. Everything that you do, whether it is in the weight room or on the field, will be an individual competition. I assure you of that. You must develop that winner's edge and understand that every rep is now evaluated and to the winner goes the spoils (playing time).

Playing collegiate sports will mentally challenge you. You must think fast and think on your feet. Players must pay close attention to detail in their plays. You must adjust quickly. Player to player communication is essential, especially for an offensive lineman. This was a big change from high school. You must now think and act quickly, make changes, and use all your energy against a possibly superior opponent. When you are mentally a step behind, you will physically be a step behind. For that, I am sure. You cannot play if you are not mentally prepared.

When you first start out, not only are you physically drained, but mentally exhausted. Sometimes the play names are so long, it is a wonder how the quarterback can relay the play to the team in the huddle. And in the game today, most plays are called at the line of scrimmage. It just adds to the overwhelming feeling of pressure about everything.

Always remember that promises and guarantees made in the recruiting process are probably empty promises. You can close your eyes and wish upon that star and dream, but thinking that your dreams will always come true is just nonsense. You must earn everything. By the way, you might as well learn this as soon as possible, because it will be true in just about every facet of your life. The same rules will apply in the world of business after your playing days are over. You must earn everything!

Tip Sheet #3

It is all about effort and attitude. Never forget that.

Some things to think about:

- *Work hard and possess a great winner's attitude and you will be successful.*
- *Never take a play off. Never duck a difficult situation on the job. Give your best effort on every play.*
- *It is easy to be just OK. Losers accept mediocrity. Winners always strive for excellence. You can never be happy with only being satisfactory. Being great takes hard work.*
- *Learn how to communicate. Successful players and successful people in business are excellent communicators.*
- *Seek honesty from people and be able to take it.*
- *Accept that on every team or in every organization or business, you usually start at the bottom of the depth chart.*
- *Understand that there will always be crummy jobs to do on any team or organization. Someone must do them. Be that person who does not hide from the*

unglamourous jobs.

- *You and only you can determine your attitude. Choose to be positive.*
- *Surround yourself with positive people. Misery loves company. This is the "dark side." Stay in the light.*
- *Be that person who your coach or your boss can always count on.*

◇

Chapter Three

Although this is the third rule in my commandment sequence, it might be the most important rule of life. And you cannot go wrong if you follow this rule. I have the unique experience of seeing how this rule plays out on both the athletic field and in life. As a player, I lived it. I lived it at as a coach and I lived it as a leader, the person in charge of not only an individual school but an entire school district.

It is a rule that will probably determine your playing time on your team, in your career, and in your promotional pathway. No one is going to promote someone with a poor attitude and a poor work ethic. Let us look at how this rule applies to one as a player and as a worker in your career.

As a player, it is essential that you exert your maximum effort on every play. You cannot take plays off. During practice, you cannot make that secret contract with the player across from you. You know that unspoken agreement to not make the other person look bad? You may have formalized this agreement in such a way that you take turns making each other look good. When you practice like this, how do you expect to get better? You must push each other on the practice field and in the weight room. You will never get better if you do not practice this. As a player, it took me a while to understand this. When I started my career, I hit the field running. As a player, what did I not understand?

This is a simple question to answer now. It took me a while to mature and maybe that is what college is all about. It gives you an opportunity to mature in a relatively emotionally safe environment. No one wants to think of him or herself as immature, but I believe that most college athletes are, in fact, immature and most people need this time to grow up. That is a tough concept to grasp. When I was 18, I thought I was "Mr. Mature." Boy, that was a joke. I wish I could do it all over again!

You cannot cut corners if you expect to achieve greatness. That is a fact. They do not pave avenues of excellence with good intentions.

Sometimes, you can physically try your best, and your best is just not good enough. Give your best each practice and you can rest peacefully at night. Sometimes, you just do not know what it means to give your best. Your coaches must help you understand this and ultimately build in you the ability to give your best effort at every play. Successful coaches can do this. Mediocre or poor coaches cannot.

The ability to do this starts with communication. And yes, you have a responsibility to communicate with your coach. Of course, the coach must make you feel comfortable in this communication pathway. I think this is the place where bad feelings start; the inability to communicate. My position coach just needed to tell me where I stood. It always seemed that I was in a guessing game.

I have tried to take that piece of knowledge with me throughout my career and life. Whenever I am in a leadership role, I attempt to communicate honestly with my team, whatever that team may be. This is not an easy skill to master and I am still learning. Everyone needs to understand his or her role and what needs to be done to change it. You need to know what you need to do to get that promotion either on the field or in the corporate environment.

Let us assume that your communication pathway is great with your position coach or your boss. You clamor for honesty. You want to know where you stand. That is a fair request. But can you take the truth? I have found that many people who seek this candor and when he or she gets it, he or she cannot deal with it. So, be careful what you wish for. My point here is that no matter what subordinate position you may be in, prepare yourself to deal with honest feedback and assessments. This is a tough skill to master, but one that you will be called upon to use throughout life. It goes back to maturity. Grow up and learn to deal with it.

It is essential that you never forget that the rookies in every program get the crummy jobs to do. Unfortunately, you will see this sort of pecking order in almost every aspect of life. You always must work your way up from the bottom. Be patient. It is a rarity that someone new to the team starts out as the star.

I can readily recall two of these crummy tasks that the rookies had to perform on my college football team. The first of these crummy tasks had very little to do with football. Each day four freshmen, rotationally, had to "drag the field" to remove the moisture from it. We had natural turf practice fields, and being in the humid south, a layer of moisture would greet us every morning on the grass. In pairs, before practice, we had to walk the field dragging these long garden hoses across the top of the grass. This dragging action caused the moisture to rise off the grass and quickly evaporate. We performed this job about 6:00 am daily during summer camp. Let me assure you; it was a pain in the butt. But someone had to do it. And you realize that the veteran members of the team had to do this same grunt work at one time. It became a rite of passage. Deal with it.

The second job that we had to do as first year linemen was to go under the bleachers and catch the pre-practice kicks taken by the placekickers on the game field. Just visualize the biggest people on the team crawling around under the end zone bleachers fielding these kicks. It got to a point where we could hear the coach coming to our locker room by his cleats on the concrete, and then we would run and hide to avoid this task. It had to be comical watching these big guys, seeking cover to avoid this pain in the butt task. Through the years, we laughed about it. On our team, it was just another rite of passage. Someone must be at the bottom of the totem pole.

Six months ago, I was the big man on campus. Now, I am scurrying around under a bleacher fielding footballs. It took a lot mentally to get used to this. All of this was part of the maturation process. It was just like the military. One had to be broken down before they could build you up to be part of your new team. Old habits had to die and new ones had to be instilled.

I was not prepared mentally for this process. I understood the physical growth process but wrestled with the mental aspect of this growth process.

Another bit of culture shock was when it was time for them to issue equipment. As the star in high school, they issued me the newest and the best equipment. As a freshman in college, they issued me the worst. Of course, it was safe and acceptable, but it was something that I was not used to. Perhaps in some of the bigger programs, this would be irrelevant, but it was not irrelevant to me. I can remember sitting at my locker after getting my first equipment and looking at it and thinking about how "crappy" it looked. It was depressing. And yes, it was another part of mentally breaking the high school superstar down. There is a pecking order to it all. You need to be patient and remember that patience is a virtue. I get it now. I did not get it then.

Physical effort is not that tough to change. Once you understand what your coaches or your boss expects from you, hopefully you can turn on your switch and physically perform. It is much harder to turn that mental switch on. To compete at a higher level, you need a certain amount of mental toughness. Some people are just not mentally tough. The entire process is like a filter. Those that are not mentally tough enough may never see the field.

One must always give one's best effort. To accompany this great effort, one needs a great attitude. And remember this; you get to choose your attitude every day. Before your feet hit the floor as you leave your bed, you and only you can control the attitude that you are going to bring to the job that day. And for the college athlete, the job is fulfilling your responsibilities as a player on your team.

Never forget that you say more with your

body language than with your mouth. No coach or boss wants to look at a pouting face all day. A boss or coach does not want to see the rolling of the eyes or mumbling under one's breath. I was not an eye roller or one that mumbles, but I am sure my position coach knew my unhappiness just by looking at me. He was wrong for not calling me out on it, yet I was wrong for letting it show. Who could argue that a player wants to play? That is a good thing. Showing discontent is bad. This is where it is essential that a good communication channel exists. You must nip attitudinal problems in the bud. My position coach, who I both liked and respected, needed to communicate. It sounds so simple, yet it is not. Go figure.

Misery loves company. The worst thing that can happen is that you become part of the group of players in the locker room that sit around all day complaining. This is just wasted energy and emotion. Collectively, your negative energy will feed off one another and do no one any good. It is easy to find others in the same situation that you may be in and join them.

The internal complaining and bitching and bellyaching about the coaches or others will do you no good. This is especially deleterious when these same people are your friends away from team activities. Then the bitching and moaning may become almost 24 /7. When this happens, it is time to break away from those people, or perhaps it may be time to move on. We will talk about that later.

Self-pity is just a wasted emotion. I spent a great deal of time on the "pity pot" early in my collegiate career. If I worked harder and perhaps exhibited a better attitude, I may have played more. I believe you can overcome some physical limitations by hard work possessing that energizing attitude.

As a principal and a superintendent of schools, I had the responsibility of hiring many people for many jobs. I hired teachers, principals, custodians, paraprofessionals, secretaries, and assistant superintendents. You name the position in the school and I hired people to fill those vacant jobs.

I can recall hiring teachers by applying some sophisticated rubric that I had developed. This rubric focused on their content knowledge, pedagogical skills, experience, and potential. I was constantly changing my template. Several years before the end of my career, I realized all my work in this area was an enormous waste of time. Somehow, I had to figure out who was going to work the hardest and who was going to have that positive, enthusiastic "can-do" attitude. I needed no more people telling me it was raining outside. Just like Noah, I needed people who were going to help me build that ark. Over my years, I became pretty good at reading people in the first 30 seconds of my initial meeting with them. I worked hard at developing this sixth sense.

I also asked myself when interviewing a candidate, can I count on this person? Yes, I needed people that were going to be there with me when the storm hit. Storms always hit. When I was coaching, I needed to know the people who were going to rise to the occasion when we were fourteen points down in the fourth quarter.

I could probably end my book here. If you work hard and have a great attitude, you will probably be a success. Yes, it is easier said than done. I encourage you to read on, because some rules that I will cover might give you some hints on how to enhance your superior attitude and tireless work ethic.

Tip Sheet #4

Internal politics exist in all organizations. Teams are no exception. You must learn how the system works. It is time to check your naivete at the door.

Some things to think about:

- *Internal organizational politics is everywhere. Get used to it!*
- *When you start out, keep your eyes and ears open and your mouth shut. Do not enter an organization as a big mouth know- it- all. If you do, you will fail.*
- *Always be mindful and respectful of race, ethnicity, and gender.*
- *Outstanding performances are hard to ignore. Exceed expectations if you wish to get noticed.*
- *Bosses (or coaches) rarely like to admit his or her mistakes.*
- *Learn to advocate for yourself.*
- *Communicate, communicate, and communicate some more.*
- *Be humble and learn how to express your gratitude to people.*
- *Know that "butt kissing" makes the*

world go around. You do not have to like it, but successful people learn how to do it.

- *Before you sign on any dotted line, learn the culture of the school or organization.*
- *Understand your personal needs.*
- *Develop additional skills and learn other people's jobs. The more you can do to help the team or business, the more valuable you will be.*
- *Be kind to everyone. You never know when you will need someone's help. No one can exist on an island.*

Chapter Four

Learn how the specific political system works in your organization or team. Each organization and yes, each team is different. Figure it out as soon as possible and learn how to play the game.

That is right. You are entering a new political arena. Once again, it is grow-up time. Take your time and observe how things work. Know who is important. Know the power brokers. Sometimes, the boss does not hold the true power in an organization. Learn who controls access to the power brokers.

Organizational politics may not be new to you. You probably have been dealing with it in your high school and on your high school team. For example, maybe your high school coach's son played on the team. Do not kid yourself. He was going to play. I am sure of that. No matter who was next up for the starting position, the coach's son was going to have a leg up on others. That is the way the world just works. This situation can be more harmful when the son is just not that good and other players at the same position are clearly more skilled. The situation becomes easier to understand when the coach's son is an outstanding athlete who should be on the field. The rumors will kill a team.

Likewise, I have been part of a team where the community thought that one player played over another because of the color of his skin. Although this is laughable, it happens. I doubt any coach operates in that manner. Coaches want to win and it does not matter what the player looks like. However, misperceptions and lies, just like vicious rumors, can kill a team. If people tell or hear a lie long enough, they may soon believe it.

On the college level, you may feel some of this politics differently. For example, you travel to another state to play and study. Some people have argued that the in-state player has a leg up on any out-of-state competition. As ridiculous as this sounds, I think it happens. Every coaching decision has implications. The formula for success is simple. You need to recruit players that are as good as, if not better than, your opponents. Then, once you get the player on campus, coach him up to compete. It is hard to win with weak players. Recruiting becomes the foundation for success. Some very successful college coaches are poor on the field coaches, yet are excellent recruiters. You quickly learn that.

The ranking systems that attach grades and stars to players coming out of high school have taken on a life of their own. There are even polls today that affix these same "star" grades to freshmen in high school. And the funny thing is that once they assign these grades and stars, they rarely change.

Hypothetically, you are a three-star recruit. You arrive on campus to find that your coaches have recruited a five-star player at your position. That five-star recruit will get every chance to win that starting job over you. College coaches dislike admitting their mistakes and they will force feed that five-star recruit no matter what. If you are that three-star recruit, can you weather that storm?

If you want to stay in that program, I hope you can deal with it. I like to believe that true talent will rise to the top no matter what happens. The same thing happens in professional athletics. The guy with the biggest contract will get every opportunity to play over a lesser paid athlete. Winning cures everything for almost everybody. Never forget that.

If you hang around long enough, you will also see the time when the team builds and plays for the future. I believe this happened to me. Without a doubt, I was not ready to contribute as a freshman. During my sophomore and junior season, I became bigger and stronger and progressed and saw more playing time. I returned for my senior season full of enthusiasm and hope. My expectations blew up on me when I woke up and the sophomore behind me on the depth chart was taking my place. I get it. The staff would not waste precious snaps on a guy who was now on the clock to graduate and leave. We were similar in ability. Playing the sophomore only made sense to the staff.

Building and maintaining a team is a cyclical event that forces the staff to juggle many balls in the air at once. Although you always want to win today, you must always keep your eye on the future. Retrospectively I get it. I had a successful coaching career and probably would have done the same thing. However, realizing and internalizing this concept years after experiencing it does not take the sting away. This is where communication by my position coach was lacking. Although I felt that communication was his responsibility, I should have spoken up and advocated for myself. One must learn this valuable self-advocacy lesson as soon as possible. You cannot be shy about it.

One of the worst practices I experienced was the periodic posting of the depth chart. What made this posting worse was there was no communication between the coach and the players. I can remember running to the bulletin board before practice to see if you were being promoted or demoted. How do you think that makes one feel?

I can share that it does not make you feel too good when you see you lost your job. A brief conversation between a coach and his player or a boss and his or her employee can go a long way, especially when one must give bad news. That is a lesson I took with me when I was a coach and later a school administrator. I always went and talked to my player and looked him in the eyes when he lost his job. I think it helped.

Likewise, as I made my way to hiring and promoting people, I followed the same procedure. I went face to face to deliver the bad news. No one wants to see that they did not get a promotion by reading it on a printed board of education agenda. I can also recall when I was the superintendent in my school district that one of my principals let a teacher go by notifying him in a letter in his mailbox. I assure you that never happened again. All organizations have communication leaks. I felt driven to beat the rumor mill.

And that perhaps becomes the heart and soul of this book. How much personal satisfaction are you willing to give up for that scholarship? And then you must ask yourself, was it all worth it? We will see.

I applaud every walk on that puts on a uniform in a scholarship program. I do not know how they do it. Perhaps it is just for that true love of the game. Being part of a scholarship program requires a lot of time and effort. Scholarship players are going to get the chance first before walk-ons. I realize that is just a fact of life. If you are that walk-on, you just must deal with it.

Before we move on, I want to emphasize something about your scholarship. Although you do not receive a weekly paycheck, the cost of a private university now is well over $50,000 per year. Take a minute to multiply that by four years and you see that your scholarship is worth over $200,000. If we tack on that fifth year and your scholarship can be worth over a quarter of a million dollars. It is a great deal of money. Your scholarship is a great value. Go ask some recent college graduates who are starting life with $100,000 in debt and will carry loan repayments for decades. Or go ask that high school classmate who is working two part-time jobs to put him or herself through a local college without parental finances. Many people who are working his or her butt off would welcome the chance of making $50,000 per year. Take a moment to appreciate that and yes, take a moment to be humble and grateful. As a recruited scholarship athlete, you are the lucky one. As I wallowed in self-pity about not playing enough, I sometimes forgot that.

Something you also must realize is that the college coaching profession is a coaching carousel. Winning drives everything. If you do not win enough, you get fired. And if you are winning, you are looking to move to a better professional situation.

When confronted with these situations, coaches are not thinking about their current players or recruits. They are thinking about what is best for them and their family. It may sound cold, but it is a reality. When a school replaces the head coach, the assistants usually leave too. You can read about these replacements and speculations every day in the news feeds. And once the cycle finishes for the current year, the new rumors begin for the next year. In the past, universities would wait until after the season to change the head coach. Times have changed and head football coaches are being let go during the season. The same is happening to assistant coaches. Some may never finish the year.

College assistant coaches fall into three categories. They are moving up to a bigger and better program or they are moving down just to hold on to a coaching job. The third category are coaches that are in a holding pattern for two or three years before they fall into category one or two. I bet that over the course of your four or five-year stay at your school, you will have several position coaches. There are very few coaching staffs that stay together for many years. Those days are over. So, the question becomes, how are you going to relate to this new coach? He did not recruit you. He does not know you. He does not have his favorites yet. Do not fret about this. In seemingly no time, he will have his stable of favorites. I am sure of that. Where will you land? Ingratiate yourself to this new position coach. Make it impossible for him not to recognize you and you must make it impossible for him not to bury you on the depth chart. I can just visualize your thoughts right now. I am being real.

Make that new coach, or your new boss in the corporate world never question your positive attitude or tremendous work ethic. Life rewards those that work hard with a good attitude and a demonstrated ability to get along with people. Whether you are a player reading this book or someone already in the job market, you say to yourself that you are not going to "kiss any butt." If you plan on being successful, you better learn this "butt kissing" skill quickly. Remember, teams, schools, and organizations are political machines.

Before you sign on that dotted line, get a "feel" for the environment on campus relative to the football program and scholarship athletes. Some schools will not consider you God's gift to humanity immediately because you are an athlete. Many schools periodically review the necessity for football entirely. This happened to me after my first year at William and Mary. William and Mary eventually found a competitive spot in the Football Championship Subdivision. They have gained respect in this division and people expect them to compete for a championship every year.

The College of William and Mary thinks of itself as a very serious academic institution, and it is. On campus during my time there, most non-athletes resented us. They were resentful of the financial commitment to the program. Many students and others in the academic community wanted the football money spent in academic areas. You had to live with that and you eventually learned to laugh at that. But by the same token, all the athletes seemed to "hang" together. We joined the same few fraternities and ran in the same social settings. However, this commonality self-segregated us from other students. And this self-segregation possibly limited our individual personal growth. And just like a family, you can get sick of one another and just need some personal space. Know what you need as a person. That will surely help you make any personal adjustment to college life.

I stress to fresh graduates that are entering the job market; it is not about what you know but who you know. And better still, whose butt you kiss. These folks will assert the same thing that a younger, less mature player will say. They will not kiss any butts. Well then, probably you will not land that job or get the promotion that you covet. Many times, your talent has very little to do with how you the organization views you. This is very sad, but very true. Get used to it. Businesses and organizations are powerful political machines and they can chew you up, spit you out and ultimately bury you.

Life is all about relationships. The earlier you realize this, the better off you will be. If that is the only message you take away from this book, then I will feel that I have accomplished something. Earlier, I spoke about the relationship with your position coach. There are a bunch of other people you need to build that good relationship with. Let's take a deeper look at a few of these:

Trainers: You want to stay healthy, don't you? You want to be treated in a timely fashion, right? Do not anger the training staff or all the student trainers. They stick together. Develop a relationship where they want to help you. I specifically know of a situation where a freshman was angry at the trainer and sneaked out of the dorm during camp and checked himself into a local hospital. How do you think that went over? I am not sure if he ever got out of the doghouse.

Equipment manager (including all student managers): You want good equipment, don't you? When something breaks, you want it to be fixed, right? You always want to find your things, right? You get it. Be nice to the equipment manager's team.

Secretaries: Your coach's secretary controls access and information. Never be disrespectful or act the fool to these folks. I know some coaches that would rather listen to his secretary about people than perhaps the position coach. The secretary sees everything and happily reports everything back to the boss.

Food service workers: You want to eat well, right? Be respectful and thankful. Having a good relationship will go a long way when you need a favor.

Academic advisors: You want to graduate, right? Maybe I just took a leap of faith. Let me rephrase that: You want to stay eligible, right? You want to assume that the academic advisors will treat you fairly. But that is not always the case. Their job is to make sure that the contributors are all academically eligible. Some coaches may want the recruiting mistakes to fail. All support personnel will receive the message without it being said. Because for each recruiting mistake that leaves school, it opens another scholarship to help find that next superstar.

Learn quickly who holds the power in your organization. And in that statement, I do not mean your boss, because, of course he or she holds the power. What I am talking about is that every day power that exists in every organization.

When I was a school principal, I used to ask new teachers who were the most important people in the school. They would incredulously stare at me, some thinking long and hard about my trick question. Few new teachers realized that for daily "in the trench" purposes, the principal's secretary and head custodian are the real power brokers. For these two positions can control information, access, and supplies. Yes, they can control the essential elements needed to function in a school. Do not anger these people. Yes, it is "butt kissing" time.

You always must be ready to perform. Prepare yourself everyday like it is a game day. It is essential that you bring something special to your team or business. Be versatile. Learn other skills and other people's job so you can jump in when your team needs you. For example, a good deep snapper (one who centers the ball for kicks) is worth his weight in gold. And no matter where you are, when your opportunity comes, grab it. You may never get a second chance.

Organizations and people are political entities. However, I must caution you that if you intend to swim with the sharks, you must be a shark. Organizational politics are not for everyone. Know thyself.

Tip Sheet #5

Keep your ego in check!

Some things to think about:

- *Make a good first impression. You need to be noticed positively. The adage of "you never get a second chance to make a good first impression" remains true.*
- *Make sure they notice you for all the right reasons.*
- *On all teams and in most organizations, you start at the bottom and must work your way to the top. Get used to it. Climbing that ladder is hard and can be a very slow and tedious process.*
- *In every new situation, you will start with a blank slate. What you say and do will paint that new picture of you on this blank slate. Make it a magnificent portrait of yourself.*
- *Know that they must remove team "obliterators" (those that will destroy a team from the inside) from the team or organization. Just like that, we remove deadly cancer from the body. The same can and should happen on a*

team. Never be that team obliterator.

- *Change is usually good. Learn to accept it. Throughout life, change is one constant.*
- *No one cares about your personal past performances. Your statistics are merely scrapbooking material. It is all about what have you done for me today. Live in the present.*
- *Someone is always watching you and evaluating you. Get used to it.*
- *Keep your ego in check.*
- *You must learn to work with others. Being able to collaborate on a task is essential.*
- *All leaders must make people better. Ask yourself this question: How did I inspire greatness today?*

Chapter Five

I already know you were a superstar in high school. Everyone was. When you get to the very top of the college athlete's food chain, they separated you by your recruiting stars or forty-yard dash times. For others, it is a matter of an inch or two or twenty pounds in weight. These are just some factors that go into deciding about playing time. I like to think that most coaches are going to play the person who gives the team the best opportunity to win. Let us assume that is a given. However, the aforementioned qualities might determine who gets the opportunity first. Yes, if you are the first one at the dinner table, you usually get to eat first and get fed.

I worked with a coach that I respected and viewed as an excellent coach. Yet one time he fell in love with a player's measurable statistics, not his performance. This ultimately hurt the team because I did not think this player gave us the best opportunity to win. I gave my opinion, but it was his choice and we did not win. Who knows if we would have won with the other guy, yet I would have liked to see him get his chance.

There is an important life lesson to learn in this anecdote. Learn to speak your mind in the correct way and then move on.

I can recall as a freshman, during our team drills, where we were polishing plays to be game ready, the first team offensive guard went down. The coach called for a guard to jump in and I was ready, willing, and able. I was also a nervous wreck. I was getting my first chance. And as my fate would have it, I jumped offsides. They whistled the play dead. They quickly banished me from taking the snaps. Of course, I was not physically or mentally ready to take the snaps. However, any hope that I had just flew out of the window. They buried me.

I remember when a freshman lineman sent a coach, who was holding a blocking dummy, flying during individual drills. Everyone was watching, and this freshman became the star for the week. He also got every quality snap in practice. I am not saying he did not deserve the snaps because he did. Unlike me, he seized the opportunity to be noticed, and it paid huge dividends for him. Good for him. I was not mentally ready. He was. So, the moral of this story is that you always must be physically and mentally ready because you never know when you get that chance to be noticed. Your goal is to be noticed positively.

I must also relate another story to you from my coaching background. As a young coach,

I had the opportunity to coach at the NCAA Division I level. I was in an entry level coaching position and part of my daily responsibility was to organize and coach the defensive scout team for our game ready players.

We were now practicing the kicking component of the game, and I meticulously lined up the scout team for our first team field goal unit. Our starting free safety was our holder for the kicks. One of my "knucklehead" scout team performers rushed the kicker like the national championship was at stake. I can close my eyes today and see him fly like a speeding missile and spear our safety /holder right in the chest as he was holding the ball. The poor holder never expected to be the target of this runaway missile. To make a long story short, he injured the holder, and he missed several weeks of game action. The coaches noticed this fool-headed human missile for all the wrong reasons. If it was not for him having NFL potential, I think they would have thrown him off the team at once. (They ultimately banished him after another incident and he never completed his first season.) They buried him on the depth chart for quite a while. And I became part of the collateral damage from his missile attack. They blamed me for not controlling him as the coach of the scout team. It was a fun day for me. (Yes, I am being sarcastic.)

The above referenced example will show you how some college coaches will tolerate just about everything to keep the star athlete. Yes, they will sell their souls to the devil for a win. Follow the money. Coaches are now paid millions of dollars to coach. Football coordinators are now paid million-dollar contracts. They will tolerate a great deal of nonsense if you can help produce wins. However, in today's world, it is harder to hide the egregious player conduct when it hits the social media circuit. Public knowledge of destructive behavior makes it harder to hide these offenses and public outcry will force the coach to deal with the issue. Believe me, I feel that most coaches would just like to close his or her eyes to this behavior and move along. For these coaches, the player's destructive behavior is not the issue. The issue becomes the public's response to this behavior.

Yet do you want to be the team's "obliterator?" You know the player that just destroys any element of team chemistry. This is the player that is merely in the game for his or her own selfish reasons. These players have little desire for team wins unless it helps his or her own personal profile. They obliterate everything. They also love company. You will recognize this person when you see him or her. Stay away! Stay far, far away from this player.

In my one and only foray into coaching at the NCAA level, I could see this behavior first hand. It is hard to describe the feeling of sitting in a meeting room with about 20 other coaches and know that your livelihood, yes, the ability to feed your family, is based upon an 18-year-old's behavior and ultimate performance. The coach's career is at risk. Everyone knows it. Coaches need to win. It is that simple. Most will play that person who gives him the best opportunity to win, regardless of episodes of inappropriate behavior. It is a rarity that a coach at this level will stand for a principled decision. The high salaries and need to keep one's job only add to this pressure.

You will start at the bottom when you begin college athletics or a new job. I have already shared some stories that freshmen in my class had to endure. You may experience the same rookie rules and roles as you enter your profession. Expect to hold and both figuratively and literally carry the dummies.

You cannot come into any new situation with a bloated ego, no matter how good you think you are. You must learn to keep your ego in check. You must learn to be humble. Humility is a virtue for everyone.

You grow from your mistakes and losing performances. You must always be able to step back and honestly and realistically assess your performance. Do not beat yourself up when you make a mistake. Learn from it and move forward.

Stay grounded and do not read and believe

your press clippings. I am speaking of both the literal and figurative press clippings. Press clippings only make you feel good about yourself. Believe me, there is nothing wrong with feeling good about yourself, but you must keep this in a proper perspective.

Let me digress a bit because lessons in keeping one's ego in check are not just on the athletic field. I used to marvel at the new teacher that expected to start at the top. On one hand, I had to applaud them for their confidence. Yet I had to laugh at some of their silly expectations. Most first-year teachers will not get that best teaching schedule or the best classroom. Administration might not even assign you a classroom, and you may be a floating teacher. No doubt about it, it just sucks. Of course, I do not think it is right, and I tried to change some of this thinking when I became a school principal. Yet, in many districts, that is just the way it is.

And from my administrative viewpoint, it is probably the worst way to do things. New teachers should get the best classes and should never float. There are too many adjustments to make as a new teacher. You should not have to worry about pushing your supplies on a cart between teaching periods. Changing that antiquated paradigm is difficult. And when you make these changes, you will receive a blowback from your staff. They were happy doing the things like they were. No one wants to change his or her ways, even if his or her ways are wrong. Many of the adults that work in a school believe that the principal's sole job is to make the school better for the adults. Principals should be about making the school better for the kids. It is a shame that some adults just do not get this. Change is a constant in life. Get used to it.

I can also recall taking over as the head football coach in a school that had very poor practice habits and their record reflected this. They did not practice hard. When I arrived, I implemented a pre-practice regimen for skill development. One of my experienced "stars" did not see the value in this and preferred to lounge around on the blocking dummies talking to fellow players before practice. I ended this behavior immediately, and it did not sit well with him. He and I had a few other disagreements in preseason camp and I quickly eliminated him from the program. He was my team obliterator. After a long career, I have found that you just cannot work with or around these obliterators. Believe me, I tried. They must go.

Many teams, schools, or organizations continue to do things without considering if it is the right thing to do. They continue to do these things because they have always done it that way. It is ridiculous, but true. Go figure. It is important that when you enter one of these situations, do not be that know it all and rub everyone the wrong way.

It is also important, as you begin your next step in your journey, that you forget your previous statistics. They mean nothing. You begin every phase of your career with a blank slate. How you fill in the blanks on this clean slate will tell your story. This blank slate will then show your positives and your negatives. It will tell your story. Hopefully, your positives will outweigh your negatives and you will have crafted a beautiful picture of yourself on this clean slate.

You cannot embellish this story. You cannot lie your way through your career. Once again, this applies to you both on the field and in the workplace. On the field, at this next level, they film everything. I am sure you have heard this next saying frequently, "the eye in the sky does not lie." Yes, that is a fact.

Everything is recorded, and you will review every snapshot of your performance after practice. This evaluation occurs whether you like it or dislike it. Get used to it. Every encounter is a minor battle, a small competition. Are you a winner?

You will watch endless hours of your performance. You will have the capability of watching this 24 hours a day, seven days a week on your team supplied laptop or iPad. If you can watch closely and honestly process that information, you will get better. I am sure of that. It will be up to you to be honest with yourself. Your own eyes will not lie. Believe what you see, not what you want to see.

When I was the superintendent of schools in my district, I tried to take this same approach to improve teaching. I was feeling fantastic about myself and this idea. As I was tossing and turning in bed, I had a revelation. I was a successful coach. I thought I was an excellent coach. The same principles that I used to build my team were what I wanted to apply in my pursuit of a great teaching staff. When I coached, I can vividly recall sitting with an offensive tackle and slowing the film and watching this big guy's first step in every play. It is a tedious process. He and I would watch each play together, breaking his first steps down in each play, correcting what was wrong, and then practicing it. Most times, our routine worked. But it only worked because we worked hard to improve. Coachable players want to hear what you have to say and then improve. Be that coachable player.

As a progressive superintendent, I discovered extra money in the budget and bought a camera system to document classroom events. My sophisticated technology allowed me to get a 360-degree view of what was happening in that classroom. I felt it was important to see what the students were doing while the teacher was teaching. The complete picture was what I was after. I got some teaching volunteers to use this technology. I promised them that my work would only help improve instruction and not be used by me in any evaluative way.

Obviously, I was working with a mindset that everyone was looking to get better. I had hoped that I had developed a sense and spirit of trust with my staff. To make this story shorter, my teacher's union vehemently objected to my plan and sabotaged my work. The union leadership urged volunteers to withdraw from this activity. In my zeal to make this work, I forgot one important element in my plan. I did not communicate my plans and ideas to the rank and file. My damage was done. I believe that the camera still sits in storage years after I retired. I missed a wonderful opportunity. But I also made some bad assumptions. I assumed everyone wanted to get better, and I assumed I had everyone's trust. And you know what happens when you assume. Right?

No one cares about what you have done. People care about what you will do. The real question becomes, whether it is on your new team or in your new job, the mentality is, "what have you done for me lately?" What you did yesterday means nothing. What you will do today means everything, and what you do tomorrow is critical. What matters is how you are helping the team right now to win.

In business, it might be even more simple. What are you doing to make this business profitable and make more money? Ok, that might sound cold but it is a reality. In the world of the public sector, it might in fact be easier to hide from that "eye in the sky" because the public sector's bottom line is easier to hide. That is one reason it is so hard to improve teaching. No matter how one tries, I do not believe that you can quantify it. When you watch the recording, you can see yourself missing that block, dropping that ball, or tripping over the invisible "turf monster." The picture gets digitized, making it available for everyone to see. For most people in the public sector or the non-profit world, evaluation is subjective. And cynically, maybe that is why that person chose this world in which to live. In the business world, it is all about monetized results. The bottom line and how you contribute to it is easy to see.

And remember, relationships matter. No matter what career path you choose, you will probably have to work with others. Teamwork and the ability to collaborate are the cornerstones of every organization. You must get along with people and yes, you must play nicely with others in the sandbox.

Also, remember that you cannot always get your way. Life is about a series of "gives and takes." Make sure that you know how to "give."

If you become a leader on that team, and I bet you will, part of your unofficial job as a leader is to make other people better. I am sure that you have that skill. You can inspire people to achieve greatness. Will you accept that challenge?

Tip Sheet #6

You are never as good or as bad as you might think. You are never as good as your parents think.

Some things to think about:

- *Never be too impressed with how important you may think you are.*
- *Learn how to self-assess. Do not believe everything you read or hear about yourself. Stay grounded.*
- *Those close to you, like your parents and friends, must also stay grounded. Self-assessment is difficult. Perhaps it is more difficult to assess the ability of your child.*
- *Keep your social media in check. The amount of your contacts or "likes" does not define you.*
- *Understand that once you accept that scholarship and sign on that dotted line, you are working, and working is not always fun (if ever). Sometimes, people expect work to be fun. That is perhaps hopeful, but unrealistic.*
- *Try to talk to someone about your emotions. I wish my scholarship included individual counseling hours.*

- *Live in the present.*
- *Throughout your life, your relationships with people change. Your friends and colleagues will change. You need to get used to that.*
- *Always be ready to go in when you are called upon.*
- *To be successful, you must persevere. Perseverance is a quality all future employers will look for.*
- *To be a contributor to a team or an organization, you do not have to be in the limelight. The backbone of a team is many times those that are in the background.*
- *You better develop some thick skin because there will always be someone talking about you either to your face or behind your back. Unfortunately, that is just part of human nature.*
- *Be aware of, and limit, any "dump and run" tactic you may use with your loved ones. By "dump and run," I mean you place a phone call to your parents lamenting whatever just happened to you. Five minutes later, on your end, all is well. The situation you just called about now does not seem so bad. However, the stress and anxiety you just laid on your parents (or the recipient of that call) is immeasurable.*

Chapter Six

We already have learned that it is essential to keep your ego in check. And coming out of perhaps a small high school in a small state, you may believe that you are "all-world." Let me assure you, you are not that good. Remember that there is or will be someone better. Previously, I asked you to be humble and practice humility. You need to internalize this. This quality may, over the long term, define you. And lack of humility can rapidly bring you down.

One defines being humble, by most online dictionaries, as the low estimate of one's self importance. Most people use it as an adjective to describe a personal trait. You have all seen that post-game interview with the star quarterback that deflects all the attention from himself to his teammates. He praises his offensive line and speaks of the great catches made by his receivers. If he is feeling very benevolent, he may point out the brilliant game plan developed by his coaches. He is being humble. We describe humility as the absence of vanity or excessive pride. Great teammates are humble. To be blunt, you are not that important. Get that into your head.

You need to stay grounded. You cannot believe your newspaper clippings. They mean nothing. Perhaps I should not say that. They mean something. They make you and your parents feel good. And we all need to feel good about ourselves. One day, twenty years in the future, you may look back on them. Today, I buried my scrapbooks deep in my daughter's cellar. I only look at them when I am changing residences and now, I believe they could stay hidden forever. I have little desire to go back down my memory lane. I have probably taken a serious look at these books twice in the last fifty years. But if you believe all the great things that are said about you, you are kidding yourself.

Learn to live in the present. The past is gone, and the future has yet to occur. This may be one of the most important lessons you can take from this book.

Likewise, the number of your social media contacts does not define who you are. You are not a better player or a better person because of the number of your "likes." Life does not work that way. Likely, you will not end up being a well-paid social media influencer. And as you move to this next level of competition, not a single person is going to care about these things.

I used to keep a box of all the letters that I received from college recruiters. That box was impressive. Now and then, I would look at it and it would impress me. I used to laugh at some schools that sent me letters because I felt as though my talent was above them. I was clearly not operating in the present or, for that matter, reality. My mindset was closed and immature. The phone calls I received from some of the "big time" coaches were impressive. Of course, they made me feel good. And of course, my parents felt good. These calls and letters did not make me a better player. They just unrealistically inflated my head. I convinced myself that I was going to go to William and Mary and be a big star, when in the end I was nothing but depth for them. Of course, all teams need reliable second and third teamers, but that would not be me.

The Ivy League heavily recruited me. Retrospectively, maybe one of these schools should have been my landing spot. To this day, I question my selection of William and Mary. The thought of that full scholarship enamored me. The Ivy League schools could only offer financial aid based upon need and although I was from a middle-class family, I would not qualify for any aid. It was unfortunate because they were elite schools with beautiful campuses and excellent coaches. These schools were also close to home. I never realized how important that my proximity to home would be.

At that immature part of my life, I only possessed a small understanding of humility. I can recall one evening, as the recruiting process was winding down, I received a call from a coach from Princeton. I had just about decided to attend William and Mary and I felt I was now "being bothered." Bothered by Princeton? Listen to me, who the hell was I? I was not very humble. I needed a big kick in the butt. As I was coming to the phone, I told my dad I was going to use this opportunity to tell the coach I was not interested in Princeton. When I got to the phone, before I could get my declination speech out of my mouth, the coach told me he could no longer recruit me. They could not get me into Princeton academically. Wow! Me? The all-time best student-athlete? Well, it would be their loss, so I supposed. I wish I recalled that coach's name because I owe him a big thank you. He started my humbling process. I was learning humility, and I was learning this lesson quickly.

I never realized how my athletic success affected my relationship with my friends. Things changed. I just assumed that they were jealous of me and they could not deal with my success. They were talented athletes too. I was just perhaps a little bigger and stronger. The years passed, and we lost all contact. Of course, things change. I get that. But in our relationships, who changed? Did my friends change or did I? Of course, we both changed. Our lives turned in different directions. I just learned another lesson in humility. Too bad I did not realize it sooner. Believe it or not, I would somehow like to reconnect with some of these friends. I remain saddened by the deterioration of our relationships. I take full responsibility for that.

This rule also pertains to your parents or loved ones. Take my word for it. They think you are better than you are. For me, my parents lived vicariously through me during this exciting period of my life. My parents were extremely supportive. During my high school years, they were involved in all aspects of the booster club and never missed a game. During my college years, they tried to attend every game. It troubled me they put this effort into my career, only to watch me mostly sit on the bench. I do not know if they ever felt the emotional pain that I felt by not playing. Maybe they did, but they never showed it. I am sure they hurt too.

We never talked about it. It was that proverbial enormous elephant that sat in every room. It is unfortunate that my father could never talk about his emotions. And on the opposite end of that spectrum, my mother only saw things through those rose-colored glasses, especially when those things were about her son.

We all marched on through my four years of being on the team and relished every time I got some significant minutes in a game. I played in an era before the cable television explosion and I know that when they were not there in person; they sat glued to the television, waiting for the score to appear. I know that they also looked forward to my call after the game. On these calls, it was hard for me not to show my dejection, even though we may have won the game. I was not as mature as I thought. Many times, I put my playing time ahead of the team's success. Shame on me. Learning humility is a process. Likewise, growing up is a process and we all do it at different times and rates of speed. Some folks just never grow up. Somehow, my parents weathered these calls. I do not know how. I became a master of the tactic of dumping and running on my parents. Looking back, I know I mentally tortured them. Why couldn't we talk about this? Who knows?

I was lucky enough to enjoy my parents' support as I entered the coaching game. Thankfully, in this aspcct of my life, we all enjoyed more success.

It was easy to learn from this experience. Somehow, I could suppress my bitterness at the game and returned to enjoying the football experience. I could also grow up.

And yes, when I became a coach, I could now look back and more fully understand the decisions that my college coaches made. Maturity goes a long way.

I must digress here to talk a bit about social media. I know I would be foolish telling everyone to reduce your social media contacts. We live our life by Facebook, Twitter, and Instagram and by the time that I publish this book, there may well be several more applications that I should list. But here is my question. Is your skin thick enough that what people say about you on these apps will not bother you? Let us assume you are the deep snapper for punts and extra points. 99% of the time, it is an extremely anonymous position. Nobody knows who is doing this job and nobody cares until there is a problem. Now the game is on the line and you blow it. Your team loses and everyone in the world blames you. The social media network lights up, looking to run you out of town. Some players, after a big mistake, have received death threats following the game. That is horrendous, but it still is a fact. Can you take it? How are you going to deal with it? Think about it.

How are your parents, relatives, and friends going to react to this public criticism of you? It is going to rip their insides apart. It is easy for everyone to accept all the accolades and glory, but can they accept the criticisms? Who knows?

The same paradigm exists in your career. I had to ban my family from reading local forums when I became principal and later superintendent. I can vividly recall the look on my wife's face when she read a local blog comprising those that were publicly unhappy with my performance. Her family bombarded her with calls, sharing all the comments pointing out all my warts. These comments hurt her more than they hurt me. I knew what was coming and knew that many disgruntled and unhappy people just hide behind these anonymous forums. Her life became easier when she and her family stopped venturing into these sites. People liked to dump their unhappiness with me on her doorstep. She too, just like my parents, fell victim to the "dump and run."

Life has a funny way of always moving forward. I made sure that I did not make the same mistake with my children. Believe me, not getting caught up in your child's success is hard to do. Likewise, not getting caught up in their trials and tribulations, and yes, their failures, might even be harder to do. You will find as a parent that when your child hurts, you hurt. It is extremely hard to separate that.

I can recall, later in my college career, my father wanted to meet with my coach and obviously try to understand why I was not playing. Thankfully, I talked him out of this. It would have been a terrible mistake. I knew why I was not starting. I was not better than my teammates who were starting. As much as I wanted to deny this, I knew it. I saw it every day. My father was just hurting for me. I knew that. And I appreciated it. It was just a no-win situation for me, or so I thought.

I can look back now and savor my Senior Day Game, where my parents escorted me on the field. It was a genuine sense of accomplishment for me and I think also for them. I persevered and we all now know how important perseverance is for success. For all of us, it was a culmination of four tough years. Through my experience, perhaps I grew more than others.

My parents are now both deceased and I am still disappointed that we could never sit and reminisce and share more of those cheerful stories. Yes, there were many of these types of tales. However, my discontent with not playing overshadowed my four-year career.

I hope you notice that I never thought that I did not contribute to the team because I did. Perhaps it just took too long to see my contribution. I tried to remain a hard worker with a respectful attitude, although I look back now and know that I could have worked harder on keeping that positive attitude.

In football, only eleven players can play at a time and yet the roster held almost 100 players. The day-to-day grind rides on the backs of players like me. These players are the ones that come to practice every day and do the best that they can do. Of course, players like me contribute to the success or failure of any team.

It is hard to realize this when you are going through it. And on the job, you too should realize that no matter where you are in the company's pecking order, you contribute.

Through it all, my experience obviously robbed me of the joy I received from playing the game. Luckily, I could recapture some of this joy through my coaching experience. I got that second chance to love and appreciate the game.

Tip Sheet #7

You are finally on your own. Home is in your rearview mirror. Love is grand, but....

Some things to think about:

- *Always know thyself.*
- *Never hesitate to talk to someone or seek outside help. Sometimes one just needs some outside independent person to serve as a sounding board.*
- *You may have to learn to hear things you may not want to hear. Do not seek honesty if you cannot deal with honesty.*
- *Sometimes you just need some "tough love."*
- *Wherever you are, find a niche of people with common interests.*
- *Never forget that misery loves company. Associate yourself with positive people with winning attitudes. You know who they are.*
- *Maintaining any long-distance relationship is hard work. Know that this relationship can be a distraction to you on your mission.*
- *Everything in life is situational. You will*

need to respond differently in different situations. I can say the same about leadership. Good leaders are situational leaders.

- *Always be ready to make half-time, game -day adjustments to your life plan.*

Chapter Seven

I previously told you I came from a home with very supportive parents. By many people's standards, one would probably consider me spoiled. But I had and still have a solid work ethic. It is one thing I am so proud of with my own grown children. I think my wife and I instilled this powerful work ethic and drive. I worked in some capacity since I was probably about ten years old, doing my daily paper route. Likewise, I can recall my dad chewing my butt off when a leaf would blow back onto the lawn that I just raked. You get my point.

But saying all of that, I could not wait to leave home. I was big and bad and wanted to be on my own. I was sure it would be a breeze. Let me succinctly say my adjustment to being away from home was difficult.

I knew in my college search; I wanted to be away, yet also wanted to be close enough to get home for a quick weekend if needed. On this topic, my mind was very far from reality. Throughout my four years there, I can probably count on one hand these quick weekend getaways. They never occurred. Yes, I was away and, for most, I believe that once you go away to college, you never really go home again to stay. You will visit, but once you have experienced life on your own, you will always want to be on your own.

That was one of the driving influences in my selection of William and Mary. From my home to the center of campus was probably a seven-hour car ride. Although the trip could be stressful and tiring, I could reasonably do the trip on a weekend.

One school that enthusiastically pursued me was the University of New Mexico. Why they were so enamored with me, I will never understand. Go figure. The coach told me some players were skiing while others were lounging by the pool. He was selling me on the climate.

I look back and chuckle about these conversations. I would have made a huge mistake choosing New Mexico. The pursuit was flattering, but I did not know myself. If I had a hard time adjusting to William and Mary, what would have happened if I made the trip to New Mexico? Can you imagine this homesick kid from New Jersey surviving in New Mexico? It would have turned into a wasted year of my life, because I am sure I would have been home by October 1st. No matter how young you might be, try not to waste a year in your life. You only have so many. And when I played, there was no such thing as a transfer portal. Of course, today it is easier to adjust to what you may think is a poor decision. But I laugh at those who play at three of four different schools in one's career. Perhaps his or her unhappiness has nothing to do with the chosen school but about him or her as a person and athlete.

You need to really know yourself. Peel back many of the layers of emotions that make up your character and do a good self-assessment. Before you make your decision about relocating, see if you can do it. You cannot kid yourself on this one, and it is easy to do. Have you ever been away from home before? How did it go for you?

I really did not know myself. I never mentally prepared to leave home. And some experts may argue that you probably cannot mentally prepare yourself for this transition. At least think about it. Of course, social media and cell phones make it easier to stay connected. Before current technology, because of the expense, my parents allowed me one phone call a week. Sounds incredible today, but that was true. I still needed to be connected. I still needed that umbilical cord to home.

And this plagued me with embarrassment for many years of my life. I viewed this as a weakness and I used to feel bad about it. I already said I could have used a counselor. I would never have thought of talking about this to a coach. They would have laughed me off campus. I could let no one destroy my "macho" image in my mind or the mind of others.

You need to think long and hard about this. Even today, I marvel at how many youngsters make this transition so easily.

I guess that there truly is a God because on this one night, he or she clearly had a guiding hand in my future. I look back now and find this story funny, but believe me, when I was going through it, there was no humor. After about three weeks into my freshman year training camp, I had hit rock bottom. For summer training, they housed the team together in one specific dormitory. I can recall after lights out sneaking out to find an isolated pay phone. I needed to assure myself that no one was going to overhear my conversation. Once again, try to think of life without cell phones. I found this phone and gathered my courage as I placed my coins into the coin slot. Strangely, my dad picked up the phone. For our house, this was an oddity. Dad never answered the phone. I can recall watching him sitting in the living room, ignoring the phone as it rang on. For whatever reason, he picked up the phone. Mom was out doing something. I skipped all pleasantries and got right to my point. I begged him to please pick me up. I thought I knew that this place was not for me. I had enough. I believed I was physically and mentally spent.

He listened attentively and when I was done; he told me that no way he was going to pick me up. However, he let me have one lifeline and he told me that if I felt the same way in three weeks, he would consider it. I knew if mom was home, the car would have left the driveway to pick me up that night. And obviously at the end of the three-week period that he gave me, things had turned around. He tested my mental toughness. I survived. There was no way I was going to throw away my hard work now. I would reassess my life at a later point. Yes, there is a God. I doubted that no more.

Life works in funny ways. My youngest daughter had the same experiences that I had starting her freshmen year away from home. My wife and I were now on the receiving end of those rough phone calls. I used the same psychology on her that my father used on me. We kept her "glued" together until she found her footing. We did not let her come home for weekend visits. Just like her father, at this stage in her life, it was now growing up time.

What saved her was she found a niche on her campus. She could make friends with people with a common interest. Any time you start a new phase of life, such as a new job, you need to find that niche where you can comfortably hang your hat. Most everyone needs some support.

I also feel strongly that you must get your mind on something other than your own personal misery. I used to tell her that when she felt homesick to go to the gym and work out and then study. Two positive activities that will keep your mind and body busy.

Misery loves company and you must work at not finding more miserable people where you can wallow collectively in your sorrow. That is not a winning effort. Work to surround yourself with people with winning attitudes. That is a lesson to last a lifetime. Unfortunately, when I was going through this transition, I found teammates who were as miserable as me. This was not a good move, for obvious reasons.

Of course, I had to make my transition more difficult because I was "in love." I left home trying to maintain a long-distance relationship with my girlfriend. Because this is not a mystery book, I will share with you now that we survived as a couple. We married soon after graduation and celebrated our 45th. anniversary this past year. My wife graduated from Rutgers. I think we both look back on this and wonder how we survived this separation.

And during my playing career we played Rutgers twice, losing both times. She still reminds me of this, but I know in one game "they robbed us." If I was on social media now, this would rate a LOL.

I believe that everyone in this world has a soulmate. We just found each other in our junior year in high school. However, neither one of us will kid ourselves. Maintaining this relationship negatively affected our college years. I think it hurt both of us academically and I think it hurt me athletically. And of course, it negatively affected our emotional health. We survived as a couple. We are the exception, not the rule.

So, what am I saying? It is quite simple. Having that significant other somewhere else will affect you. It will affect all facets of your life. For that, I am sure. If this relationship is important to you and you feel that this is the "one," you must factor this relationship and your feelings into your college selection decision. Do a bit of a self-analysis. And you must be honest with yourself and honest with your significant other. This is an easy time to think that you are "big and bad," but this false bravado could very well end up being your demise.

Unfortunately, I do not have the magic answer for you. My future wife and I tried saying goodbye and letting the chips fall where they may. It did not work that way for us. We fought for our relationship. However, it took its toll on both of us. And yet, ultimately, dealing with this separation could have strengthened our relationship. Who knows?

If you are in my situation, what will you do? Whatever your deicide, it will affect you and must be a factor in your decision making. Just do not hide from it and pretend it will not matter because it will. You may face a similar decision when you are in the workforce. What are you going to do when your boss calls you into the office and tells you are being transferred to a new location? And this conversation occurs just as you bought that engagement ring for your lady. You know that you have a bright future in this company and you also know that to move up your career ladder, you must go where the job takes you. What is going to happen? It is time for your relationship to be tested. Will she move with you? Will you keep your job? These are tough questions and are ultimately life changing questions. You should not and cannot make this decision with only your heart. Please use your brain using a future driven lens.

Let us keep this conversation going. In two-career families, one career will ultimately take a priority. You are lying to yourself and each other if you think you will value both careers equally. And valuing a career is not always about money. Of course, money is critical, but you cannot undervalue your happiness and the happiness of your significant other. I was extremely fortunate that my wife sacrificed for me. Although she was very skilled and competent in her field, she consciously allowed her career to take a backseat to mine. Yes, I was lucky. And yes, we turned out to be one of those forever soulmates that I spoke of.

Everything in life is situational. You must respond to every situation differently. You always must have your eyes wide open. Please do not forget this concept when someone thrusts you into leadership roles. You must be a situational leader, always leading in the manner that is dictated by each situation.

Think of situational leadership like building a game plan. We build each game plan on the opponent's strengths and weaknesses. One common game plan will not work for each opponent. If you tried this method of preparation, you will lose more games than you win. Likewise, if you use the same packaged game plan for each leadership situation that confronts you, you, too, will lose in this arena. Think about how you will make those game time decisions and how you will adjust your plan accordingly. Those that cannot adjust will ultimately lose and fail.

Tip Sheet #8

Learn to take feedback like a champ

Some things to think about:

- *The way you accept feedback will be a barometer of your level of maturity.*
- *Throughout life, deal with coaches or bosses that dislike you. Although you may not like them, you need to play hard or work hard for them.*
- *Everyone wants to be treated equally. However, we cannot treat everyone the same. Get used to it. Strive for being treated fairly.*
- *No matter how down you may feel, keep an optimistic outlook. Do not pout or sulk.*
- *Your feedback is yours. It is personal. Keep it that way.*
- *No one ever wants to reward Eeyore, nor will they feel sorry for him or her.*
- *Do you really want to hear the truth? Are you sure? Because sometimes, the truth will hurt.*

Chapter Eight

I am sure that life will challenge you. Something will always test you for your strength and maturity. This test will occur when you start your college athletic career or when you start your first job. Life's failures, mistakes, and negative feedback will challenge your maturity level. Maturity and success go hand in hand. Mature people are usually more successful. I still test my maturity today.

You need to be coached hard. And that coaching could be from your position coach on the field or your direct supervisor or manager on the job. If a coach does not coach you hard, I would consider that coach negligent. If that coach is not pushing you, then he or she is not doing his or her job. And part of that hard coaching is for you to accept corrections and criticism like a champ.

Please do not infer that I mean hard coaching is to be abusive. Because that too is negligent. Coaches must be positive and coach their players "up." And honestly, not all coaches are positive or good. Dealing with these bad coaches is part of the maturation process. I wish I could promise you that all your coaches, managers and bosses are good.

I wish I could promise you that you will always have fun on the athletic field or on the job. Some coaches or bosses just stink and I will promise you that somewhere in your career, you will play for or work for one of these bad coaches, managers, or bosses.

I can vividly recall a story about a manager being the real-life version of Cruella Deville. This person was just evil and enjoyed mentally torturing her direct reports. This manager set up an impossible culture in which to work and survive. She relished punishing people, especially new people. Athletic coaches can also be like that and somehow, this coach or boss will expect you to perform for them. This may sound outlandish, but it is true. As a player, regardless of the coach, push yourself to perform at your highest level. Your rewards and motivation must be internal.

Please remember your own personal feelings when you are in a position of leadership. Do not repeat the mistakes of your poor coaches or managers. I never forgot the perceived faults of my coaches and I believe that in my career, I never repeated them.

Players and people expect equity. And part of that is being treated fairly. However, we should note that treating everyone fairly does not always mean treating them equally. Some people have earned some special considerations. Get used to that.

Coaches also have favorites. That is only

human nature, so you must accept it. I bet you were a favorite of your high school coach. You had a set of skills and if you were looking to play at the next level; you had to be good. As a coach, it is easy to like talented players if he or she has the right attitude. You consistently hear about people being kept on a team because of the locker room chemistry. Likewise, you hear of people being traded or cut because they hurt the chemistry in the locker room. You need to be that player that coaches love to coach. This skill is harder to master when you are not the best player. Never forget that.

Coaches want to like the players that want to win and be successful. That is an easy marriage. Liking that pain in the neck player or worker is difficult.

There is nothing more annoying for a coach than to look at his players and see a bunch of Eeyores. You know, Winnie the Pooh's donkey friend, who always had the pouting sad face. He is pessimistic, cynical, gloomy, depressed, negative, and probably divisive. Take a moment and look at Eeyore's face and you will become depressed. In retrospect, I know that sometimes my college coach looked at me on the sideline and I am sure he saw Eeyore. I wanted to play so badly, I could express nothing but sadness, even when we were winning. This was not my expression all the time, but I knew it was there. This was a sign of my immaturity and not being prepared to get coached hard. I was more concerned with my playing time than with winning. Shame on me.

When I became a coach, I had a "no pouting" rule. I was overly sensitive to this. My team would not be a team of whiners. And I know that this rule probably cost us a game or two before that rule became part of the team's culture. It was worth it. I wanted to coach players that wanted to be coached. I wanted players who understood their role on the team and, although perhaps not happy with it, could deal with it. I wanted players who always remained positive and were ready to win whenever they were called upon.

Pouting and whining will destroy the culture of any organization. I saw this negativity firsthand when I became the principal of my school. This personal negativity affects and will hold back any organization, business, or team. I witnessed this firsthand. It is hard to change.

One way to change this on a team is to recruit only players who can possess this winning attitude. Likewise, in an organization, it is essential that you hire only those people with this attitude. And sometimes, when taking over a team, school, or organization, you must jettison those that are in your eyes unable to be coached. Now that is the real challenge! Good luck.

Keep your feedback private. As a player, this

can be hard because many times your coach will provide this feedback to you on the run and on the field. When you are in a leadership position in your career, feedback to others must always be in private. Early in my leadership career, I made this mistake, and it took me a while to dig myself out of the hole that my feedback technique put me in.

When you have any private sit downs with your coach or boss, what they say there is private. Respect that. The rest of the locker room, school, or business does not have to be brought into your feedback loop. When provided feedback and opportunities for growth, keep it private. Your personal business should not become fodder for break room discussions. Remember that misery loves company rule. Keep it private!

In these private sit-downs with your coach, I encourage you to ask questions and seek clarifications. It is essential that when you leave this meeting; you understand what they said. Personally, I recall times when I left these types of conferences, more confused than when these meetings started. It is easy to become overwhelmed with the emotions of the meeting and you cannot grasp the essence of what they said. If that happens, the meeting was a waste of time. You need to seek clarity. Ask questions until you understand the issues.

Now please do not make this one mistake that I have seen happen time and time again in my leadership roles. You and your coach or boss may never agree. That does not mean that they have not heard you or appreciate your feelings. You just disagree and ultimately if you are not the boss, you must get your head in the right place to continue to move forward.

By my senior football season, I knew I was going to coach someday, and I worked hard learning while observing. I tried to learn from others what to do and what not to do. I committed to make my time on the bench productive and useful for my future.

I can recall having to meet with one of my school players during a state championship season because I could not stand seeing his Eeyore face on the sideline. I explained to him he had a role on the team and had to accept that role if he wanted to stay on the team. If he did not stop disrupting me with his negativity, I was going to let him go. He responded how I hoped he would respond. He hung in there, practiced hard, stopped his moping, and eventually became a contributor on game day. I think for him, his championship ring may have meant a little more than what the ring meant for some of my stars. He was truly grateful. A life lesson learned. I wish I had a video history of this individual because it would serve as a training tool for future players or work colleagues.

Always remember that no coach wants to reward his or her Eeyore with playing time.

Likewise, no boss would ever think of promoting his or her own Eeyore. What type of bonus would Eeyore qualify for, especially when they award bonuses via some subjective rubric? Be smart, mature, and practical.

It is important that you learn that what you say with your body language is many times louder than what you say with your voice. Coaches and managers always read your body language. You must be attentive and alert. You say this with your eyes wide open, focused on what is being said. Lean forward and send body signals to the speaker, like a periodic nod of the head, to show that you are listening. Keep your phones tucked away. Check your social media or email at a different time. A game of Solitaire on your phone will wait for you. Nothing is more annoying than seeing people on their cell phones in the audience. I think that if I was coaching today, keeping your phones tucked away at meeting time would be a very important rule.

If you want to be coached hard, and I trust you do, you cannot have thin skin. You cannot take this hard coaching personally. A good coach or a good boss does not attack you personally. A good boss is pushing you to make you better. And if you are better, the team or company will be better. When receiving feedback, do not argue with that person. When it is feedback time, it is time for you to listen. Keep your ears open and your mouth shut. Now is not the time to become argumentative or combative. That demeanor will get you nowhere, except perhaps in the coach's or boss' doghouse. Understand that it might take some time for you to process what they said. Understanding your feedback will allow you the time to implement personal changes. Make the changes that your coach or boss suggests. That is a wise move.

When truths are told, it is hard not to want to make excuses or provide some rationale for what happened. Coaches or bosses do not have the time or the desire to hear excuses. A coach does not want to hear that the ball was slippery, which caused you to fumble. A good coach is telling you how you may have been holding the football to make it is easier to fumble. A good coach is trying to help you ensure your mistake does not happen again. Always remember that the past is gone. What you do in the present will affect the future.

Hearing the truth can hurt. I find it funny that most people clamor for the truth and when the truth comes out, he or she did not really want to hear it. Learn to accept the truth and get better because you embraced the truth. Learn how to look honestly in your mirror and see exactly who you are. And as you are looking, make sure that you look at what lies beneath the skin or that outer appearance.

Earlier in this book, I explored how difficult it is for you to evaluate your own ability. I can say the same to your parents. Your parents will also look to make excuses for your performances. It is hard being a parent. Like I previously stated, you hurt when your child hurts. It is hard for them to accept when you are playing badly or not playing at all. I am sure you already know how it feels when your mistake leads directly to a team's loss. I ask you to think how your parents must feel sitting up in the stands when you blow a game. Think of how they feel when you are being booed off the field. Think of how they feel when they are hearing all sorts of profanity directed at you.

They are being subjected to a more intense scrutiny than you. At least you can play your way out of the situation. The next time you touch the ball, you can score the winning touchdown. It is not that easy for your parents. They will sit silently in anguish. Who is there to put an arm around them or to pat them on the backside? Your teammates or a coach can help you address your pain. Who is there for your family and friends in the stands?

If you perform at a higher level, then your performance will translate into more wins for your team or more financial gains for your company. Both literally and figuratively, winning translates to higher earnings. If you cannot perform at a winning level, someone else will be and you will be out of a job. The formula is not too difficult to understand. It is simple and obvious. Do not be a blockhead.

And never pretend that you do not get it, because you do. We reward winners in all facets of life. Losers will eventually disappear.

Tip Sheet #9

There is a mental aspect to everything. Along the way, the system plays faster, both physically and mentally. You must learn how to advocate for yourself. Academics are important!

Some things to think about:

- *Everything just moves faster at the next level, including thinking. You will be required to think fast and make very few mental errors.*
- *Your activities should point towards the future. What you do today will affect what happens tomorrow.*
- *In life, you must be a quick learner.*
- *It is important to feel comfortable with your team or in your corporate environment. Never underestimate the importance of culture and climate.*
- *It is hard to meet high expectations if they have not challenged you to do so in the past.*
- *Mental toughness is critical for success.*
- *Learn to advocate for yourself.*
- *You will be driven. Regardless of your*

drive, make good decisions.

- *Choose to be happy. You and only you can control this.*
- *Explore what life holds for you. It may surprise you.*
- *The good players usually work the hardest.*
- *Never lose your competitive drive.*
- *Expect excellence of yourself and others.*

◇

Chapter Nine

There is a mental aspect to everything. Thinking faster and deeper will always be a challenge for you. This is true whether we are talking about moving up in a level of play or moving up in your chosen career path. Everything moves faster. What you once took for granted as instinct now requires you to think before you act. Be patient. Your new routines will soon become instinctual. It just may take some time. For years they have spoiled you because everything came easily to you. Everything was simple. One plus one always equaled two. You were also probably the most athletically gifted. You may have always been the biggest, strongest, or fastest. Not anymore. Now, everything seems like your first day in algebra class.

You must also possess common sense. At least I hope you do. Unfortunately, as I hired more people in my school leadership roles, I came to realize that many people were just lacking some good old common sense. That is a sad indictment, but it is true. I am convinced that you know right from wrong when you see it. You should not have to be

94

told everything. Just do the right thing!

Let us not forget the reason that you enrolled in college. You want that college degree. You want that degree to help secure your future. What you do with that degree will be up to you. Even if you are one of the very few players that will make their living playing the game for a short time, you need that degree.

Remember what I said in the first few pages of this book: your professional career will be short. There is life after football. Are you going to be prepared? We could argue all day about the value of that degree. Yes, there are a few megastars that will make tens of millions of dollars playing each year. They will not have to worry about making a living.

But I will also argue that the exact opposite, namely that there are many former players that are struggling to make a living once their playing career is over. Their big bonuses are gone. Their big game day paychecks are gone. Now what? You need to be prepared for that. I applaud the players that go back to finish their degree requirements after their playing days are over. My heart also aches for those players that totally blew their chance because they were living in some dream world.

For me, high school offensive line play was simple. You blocked the guy that was lined up across from you. Most times you over powered this person because you were just bigger or stronger. But now, moving up to the next level, everything has changed. You now have a great deal of thinking to do prior to the play ever starting. People were now changing blocking schemes based upon the alignment of the defense. Offensive plays were being called or changed at the line of scrimmage. Defenses moved prior to the play. It seemed as everyone on the line was making some call to change the play or blocking assignments based upon what the defense showed. It was eye opening.

Also, you were no longer the biggest and fastest person out there. For me, the opposite turned out to be true. I was now the smallest offensive linemen. Offensive line is a tough position to come in and play immediately because of the mental aspect of the game and the speed at which you must act. I think that it really takes a year or two in a college weight training program to bring you up to speed physically to play and contribute at this level. These were huge adjustments to make as an incoming freshman. It was very easy to be beaten both physically and mentally.

I have been told that a similar change happens when you move from the college ranks to the next level. At that level, it is not the size difference that gets you; it is the speed of the game and the speed of the players. There is also a huge, almost exponential, jump mentally. The same type of gap exists when you start that new job. You either know your field or will learn quickly what is required for you to do your job. But will you be able to do this learning both quickly and accurately? Just like in athletics, you need to find the right level of intensity in the corporate world.

Climbing the corporate ladder rapidly is not for everyone. Find your niche and be comfortable in that niche. Everyone cannot play sports professionally. Everyone cannot be a Division I college athlete. Everyone cannot occupy the corner office. Please do not forget the big fish, small pond mentality that I spoke about in my set of rules to live by. It also applies in the business world. Be comfortable in your own skin and you must feel comfortable in the right company. Never underestimate the importance of a team or corporate culture and climate. You need to fit in. I know of people who have left jobs simply for money only to regret it quickly thereafter. They only saw the dollar signs, not the other factors of a corporate culture.

It is also important to know yourself and what makes you tick. Everyone cannot manage and supervise people. There is nothing wrong with that. On the coaching level, everyone is not cut out to be that head coach. He or she may be a great offensive or defensive coordinator, yet falls flat on his or her face when they ascend to the top position.

Ok, I admit it. I have become a William and Mary snob. The College of William and Mary is a highly competitive academic school. It is not for everyone. They have their standards and live by them. You earn your grades. No one gives them to you.

For some highly competitive schools, once they admit you, the tough part is over. Of course, I am oversimplifying. Usually, once you are in, you stay until you finish your degree requirements. That is not the case at W & M. If you do not cut it academically, you are gone. They also have a strict honor code. I saw fellow students succumb to the rigid academics and unfortunately; I saw some succumb to the honor code.

Maybe I inadvertently put myself in that "no win" situation. I was in over my head athletically and I was in over my head academically. Please do shed any tears for me. I had my full college education paid for and earned my degree from one of the most prestigious schools in America. But at what cost? Ah, now that is the question.

I struggled on both fronts. And it was all about the speed of the "game." Here, the game I mean is in the classroom. I already alluded to the speed of the game on the football field. Believe me, the expectations and speed in the classroom were just as fast as the speed on the field.

When you entered the classroom, professors had a preconceived expectation of what you could do. You had to come to that first class prepared to learn. For many of my courses, there was a reading assignment that was due for that first class. That was a new paradigm that I had to adjust to. That was a new paradigm for all.

I can recall entering my college biology class on that first day. I would estimate about 300 students filled that lecture hall. On an aside, one reason I chose William and Mary was because of its relative smallness, including class size and teacher to student ratio. However, there were several courses set up as a filtration mechanism to weed out any academic pretenders. Bio 101 was one of them.

People go to William and Mary to become doctors and lawyers. I did not know what I wanted to become, which is another story I will talk about a bit later. Good old W&M was going to thin this flock early. I was a good biology student in high school and figured I would breeze through Bio 101 in college. I breezed right out of the door of Bio 101 with a big fat F. I became one of the many failures in that class. I had no clue how to study. I had no clue how to learn in a lecture hall and I had no clue about doing laboratory assignments. I just had no clue, period. I failed nothing in high school. Now I had had to deal with my first failure. It was tough for my psyche. It was also tough for my parents to comprehend this. I am sure they thought I was sitting around drinking beer all day, never studying. I was studying my butt off. I just did not know how to study.

Unfortunately, I breezed through my high

school academic career. I received A's and B's barely studying. I never really applied myself until college. I can honestly say that it took me probably a year and a half to understand how to study. To finally get it.

I followed up my first semester failure in Bio 101 with a second semester failure in an introductory math course. I continued to plod along, showing little improvement. After my freshman year, I was six credits shy of being athletically eligible for the next season. I took several courses at a school near my home in the summer to gain my eligibility. I wonder if my coaches were hoping I would not return academically, so they would save a scholarship? I proved them wrong.

However, if I was to do this all over, I would have stayed on campus for the summer. I would have gotten better academically and I would have gotten better as a player being on campus for summer activities. But if you remember from a previous rule, I was in love and home is where I wanted to be. Today, I do not think my coaches would have allowed players to take courses away from campus. However, today I could have probably taken these courses on-line.

Believe it or not, I was getting better. I was working my butt off in my local weight room and getting myself in the best shape of my life and was finally getting this academic thing. Thankfully, things were slowing down.

According to Bruce Springsteen, in one of

my favorite songs, *Rosalita*, "someday we'll look back on this and this will all seem funny." Yes, there is some truth in that statement and this anecdote will prove it. I will take some suspense out of it and tell you I never failed a course again.

However, in the fall semester of my sophomore year, they assigned me to another large lecture hall for Psychology 101. Unlike Biology, this was supposed to be "easy." It was difficult for me though. I struggled. As I already told you, I do not do large lecture classes well. The professor was reviewing a test we had just taken and announced to the class that the grades ranged from 52 to 92. When we picked up our papers at the end of class, I saw that the 52 belonged to me. Was this an error? Was this a joke? Was this some sort of psychological experiment? Believe me, I thought of all the reasons and excuses. I studied. I read the material. I just outright failed. This discouraged and humiliated me. I snuck back to my room and prayed that my roommate was not there. I can recall laying on my bed almost paralyzed by my failure on this one test. Was I the dumbest student in that class? I felt as if I was the dumbest student in William and Mary. I had returned to campus with such hope and here I go again, a big red "F." Somehow, I rebounded. I told no one of my score and plodded along and somehow, to this day, I still feel this humiliating experience. I do not think I failed another test. Perhaps I was tougher mentally than I thought.

You also must learn how to advocate for yourself. This lesson needs to be learned by everyone. Self-advocacy is important for success on the playing field or in the corporate office. If you cannot be your own advocate, you will quite possibly have a very long and anonymous career. Some of you reading this book may seek this anonymous career. But somehow, I doubt that. I will argue that a competitive athlete does not want to be anonymous. It is not part of his or her DNA. They want to rise to the top. I know I did. You must approach your professors, coaches, or bosses maturely. Learn to ask the right questions and seek the right guidance. It is essential that this "check-in" type of experience becomes a way of life for you. However, remember that this is just a check in. You cannot seek to be told everything. Many times, I had to remind my staff that reported to me that if I had to figure everything out, then perhaps I did not need them. I hope you get my point.

My outlook and life changed when I started coaching. I never felt satisfied. I was driven to be the best assistant coach on the staff. I was driven to have my unit be the best performing unit in every game. In the corporate world, you can and should still possess that drive. You want to be the best salesperson on your team. You want to be the best lawyer in your practice. You are just driven to be the best.

When I was a football position coach, I was driven to be a coordinator where I had charge of the offense or defense. It was not long after that experience that I wanted to be a head coach. I then thought that the only way to be an excellent coach was to do that at the NCAA level. And once I had the experience, I quickly learned that you could be an excellent coach at any level. Some coaches I worked with at the NCAA level were just not good coaches. I learned an excellent lesson through this experience.

When I went into school administration, my drive was similar. I started out as a curriculum supervisor and leaped to the role of assistant principal at my high school. Just like in coaching, I wanted to be the principal. Soon I became principal at my middle school and it was not long before I wanted to be back at the high school as a principal. My drive did not slow down. They soon promoted me to assistant superintendent, and I ended my career as the district's superintendent.

My point in the previous two paragraphs was not to impress you with my resume. My goal was to illustrate to you, my drive. I would have never moved through the ranks of my chosen profession if I could not advocate for myself. Young people are afraid to do this. Get over this fear and get over it quickly. You must also be your own promoter. Go out and compete for the things that you want.

There are two things that only you can

control. The first one is your attitude. You need to stay positive no matter how difficult your life seems. Second, you can control how hard you work. You need that positive attitude combined with a great work ethic and I can just about ensure your success. I developed in my hiring practices not to hire for content knowledge or skill, but to hire for attitude and work ethic. That is the only way to go. You can always coach up content or a specific skill. I am convinced now that work ethic and attitude are part of your DNA.

The good players work the hardest. The same can be said of good teachers, good principals or for that fact good corporate workers. I think I made my point. Work hard!

It is also essential here that I impress upon you that your education is never terminal. Hopefully, you are learning until the day that you die. I quickly earned my master's degree and when I was pursuing my doctorate, something beyond my control derailed me. To this day, I regret not completing my doctorate.

Retrospectively, I know that if I was moving up my career ladder today, I probably would have stalled before I reached the top because of this lack of degree. Who knows? Yet, I did not sleep through that psychology class I told you about. I learned about Abraham Maslow and the concept of self-actualization. And for me, I did not attain this level of self-actualization that earning my doctorate would have achieved. I have had few regrets in my career. This is one of them.

Let us now turn to career exploration. Once again, this discussion applies to anyone, not necessarily the athlete. There is a lot to be said for happiness. One wants to be happy in his or her chosen field. I cannot even visualize what it would be like going to work every day for forty years hating his or her job. But let us be clear on that. You cannot expect your job to be fun every day. If that is your expectation, it will disappoint you. You will have good days and bad days. That is part of a one's career. Being happy and having fun are two unique items. I have worked with some folks that cannot see the distinction. These are the people that usually end up hating his or her job.

Before or during college, explore what you want to do in life. I blew it. I came from a family where my older sister was the first person to go to college. She became a nurse. I followed her into college and became a teacher. We both had a competitive spirit and drive, and both of us moved on quickly from our entry-level positions. But my point here is that both of us fell into very traditional roles, namely a nurse and a teacher. Both careers were probably the only ones my parents knew for a college bound person. My parents were not college graduates. They believed in the traditional roles for boys and girls in that time era. She should have been a doctor and perhaps I should have been a college professor. Who knows what our lives would have been? We just did not know better. Never lose your competitive drive.

Unfortunately, our schools, both high school and university, also let us down. As a principal and superintendent, I tried to change that. For most of the kids in my schools, I feel I was successful in that regard. I taught the importance of high expectations and how to attain them. However, William and Mary prides itself in being a liberal arts university, and not one person ever spoke to me about a future career. Of course, it was my responsibility and I do not blame W &M, yet it would have been nice to have had some guidance. If opportunities for this exploration existed, I just missed them. Or perhaps I was maybe so locked into what I thought I wanted to do; I closed my mind to other possibilities. Shame on me for this behavior.

Keep an open mind and explore all your options during career exploration. Remember, your career lasts almost a lifetime. It would be nice to be prepared and it would be nice to be doing something that made you happy. Without doing this, it would be like going into a game without a game plan. Not one person would do this regarding his or her athletic competition, yet most go into life unprepared. And this unpreparedness to me just makes little sense.

A colleague of mine who worked for a large Fortune 500 company had this quote posted on her bulletin board. "Your work is a self-portrait and you must autograph it with excellence." These are impressive words to live by! Always expect excellence from yourself and others.

Tip Sheet #10

The school / coach or the employer /employee relationship is a delicate balance. Know when to pull the plug and move on.

Some things to think about:

- *Clearly understand the reasons you chose your school or business.*
- *Pick the school or job, not the boss or coach. Bosses and coaches come and go.*
- *Change is one constant you can count on.*
- *Your career, future and life can change in an instant. What happens to you with a career-ending injury? What happens if you are in a terrible car accident?*
- *The "grass is not always greener on the other side." A new school or a new job may sure look attractive, but you find out quickly it is far worse than what you left.*
- *Be cautious of parents living through their children. It happens more often than you might think. And you might not see this phenomenon until you are*

raising your own children. If you do not believe me, look around at the youth soccer fields or local dance studios because you will surely see what I mean. Also, be sure to take a good look in the mirror. Are you that person?

- *Throughout life, you will always face tough decisions. Before deciding, weigh all the pros and cons of your decision.*
- *There is a lot to be said about culture. It cannot always be about money.*
- *The school / coach balance (employee / boss) is delicate. Know when to pull the plug.*
- *Ask yourself if you are choosing the school (job) primarily for the school or for the coach (boss)?*

YOU HAVE A RIGHT TO BE HAPPY!

Chapter Ten

I know years ago, there was never a question about this. You made your decision based on the school. Of course, recruiting personalities may have played a role in your decision, but ultimately, your decision should have been about the school. Now, some high school athletes are choosing the coach over the school. I am still old-school with this question. I think one should commit to the school. Likewise, when you accept a job, you are picking a company, not your boss.

Some players will make his or her decision based upon future potential professional opportunities. Others will make this decision with NIL (name, image, likeness) and pool money possibilities. The NIL allows college athletes to be paid for the use of their name, image, or likeness. Some high school athletes and transfers are now being recruited with million-dollar NIL deals in mind. Yes, it has become a bidding war for some recruits and transfers. And for these players, as I stated earlier in the book, this book might just not be for you. Dreams have been shattered for some because of severe or career-ending injuries.

So, on second thought, perhaps my ten simple rules will be of great use to them, too.

In 2018, the NCAA created the transfer portal. This is a system where student-athletes could start the recruitment process all over again. You can find out the specific details of the portal by visiting the NCAA website. These rules continue to develop. The NCAA will now allow a onetime transfer waiver to each student athlete, which allows them to compete at his or her new school immediately.

In past years, the student-athlete had to wait a year to compete after transferring. This requirement prevented many students from considering a transfer. Few people wanted to pause his or her life for a year awaiting eligibility. The Pandemic also disrupted player eligibility and the transfer process. Graduate students can also transfer without a penalty if any eligibility remains.

Why do student-athletes transfer? There are many reasons. Considerations may include playing time, academics, campus life, geography, NIL money and more. If one is to consider transferring, one should realize the seriousness of this decision. Although some athletes have tried to make this a merry-go-round type of activity, few that take this approach are successful.

One must also take a moment and ponder the "grass is not always greener" philosophy. When you are miserable, for whatever reason, escaping the situation seems like the only way to go. And when you escape the situation and end up in a new place, you quickly realize that what you had was not so bad.

As a principal and superintendent, I used to give this advice regularly to people who I supervised. Each time a person expressed a desire to leave my school, I would sit with them and review all the positive and negative aspects of this impending decision. When you are on the precipice of leaving your school or firm, you probably feel that you could not get more miserable. However, after you leave, you quickly learn that you could get more miserable once you have settled in to your new environment.

An'd yes, many times, I would get that call from the person who left, begging me to return to my school or district. Sometimes, I would take that person back if I viewed him or her as an asset. Other times, I would stay clear of that person and his or her departure would thrill me. I just caution everyone to be careful what you wish for.

So, why didn't I transfer? That is certainly a good question and one I still think about. I think I can break it down into several categories.

First, I was ignorant of the system. I never took the responsibility for learning how to do it. It was probably a little more complicated back when I played, yet I still never researched the process. However, that did not stop me from bellyaching and complaining about how miserable I was. Perhaps I just liked to hear myself complain. Maybe I was just happy being miserable. Who knows? However, there was something in me that spoke to the fact that I made a commitment and I had to make this thing work. In situations like this; it was necessary for me just to put my head down and plug along.

Second, I was reluctant to give up my scholarship. It was extremely valuable financially to my family and me. Perhaps staying at William and Mary was purely a monetary decision. And yes, there was a source of pride in being a scholarship athlete. Would someone else have offered me a scholarship then? I wanted to believe someone would, but my lack of playing time likely caused others to rule me out. Unlike in high school, I did not have the excellent film or films to show. Although I was clearly bigger and stronger than I was in high school, people could no longer evaluate my skill. Many schools just did not embrace the entire notion of transferring like they do today. Schools were globally not leaving scholarships available for transfers in their total scholarship allotment.

Finally, and perhaps the biggest reason I did not transfer, was that I did not want to let my parents down. They would have been heartbroken. I knew it was easier for me to accept my fate for the next several years rather than face the disappointment my parents would feel if I left William and Mary. It is funny that I knew all of this without ever entering any sort of conversation with them about this. They would listen to me moan and groan, but never once did they suggest the notion of me finding a place where I might be happier.

Were they somehow vicariously living their own lives through me? Perhaps, yet I think they would sit in anguish watching my games and ultimately watch me sitting on the bench.

Always understand that you have a right to be happy. That is something that I did not fully comprehend at 20 years of age. I do not know if I even understood that at 40 or 50 years of age. My grappling with my happiness is something I still do. Go figure that one out. Perhaps I am still growing up.

Never forget the importance of the culture of your team, school, or current job. I spoke about this in the previous rule but I think it is important to repeat. Throughout your career, you may change jobs because there is a lure of more financial compensation. Then you realize the culture you left was worth a lot more than a few extra dollars in the pay envelope. Please take a moment to read this paragraph again and again. I do not want you to experience any big regrets, but sometimes, one just must learn for oneself. Never say I did not warn you.

In my career, I look back at myself as an

idea guy. A guy who would try different innovations, structures, and programs to improve my schools. Now I think that this may have all been a waste of my time. I should have spent my time building a better, more positive culture and climate for my schools and district.

Ultimately, you must know when to pull the plug. Sometimes, it is just not working where you are and there is nothing wrong with moving on. Yet, one should not make this decision cavalierly. One must make it with a great deal of thought and consideration, clearly listing all the pros and cons of you leaving or staying where you are. There is a wealth of literature on this topic. I would explore this bank of material and talk with a trusted mentor on this subject.

Chapter Eleven
Time to evaluate the game film.

So, was it worth it?

When I started this book, I was wrestling with a question that I thought about for years. I lost sleep over it as I would lie in bed thinking about this. Was it worth it? Was what worth it? Even though I played sporadically, and never started a game, was my athletic scholarship worth it? Would I have been happier playing football in college at a level where I would have been more of a contributor? That is right, no athletic scholarship but the chance to play, start and perhaps be that big man on campus once again.

At the onset of my work, I was sure of my answer. No, it was not worth it. I should have gone somewhere where I could have been on the field playing and enjoying the game. But as I dug deeper into this topic, my opinion changed.

Looking back some fifty years later, yes, going to William and Mary was well worth it. I would tell my 18-year-old self to go for it again. But go for it in the right way. The

*first thing that I had to do was grow up.
Next, I had to push myself harder
physically and mentally and attack the
game, and life, with a better attitude.
There are those words again: a better
attitude. I am convinced that everything
in life is about effort and attitude.
Sometimes you must push yourself until it
hurts physically or mentally. I did not get
this. I did not possess the mental
discipline. It was really all about me. I
never figured that out. I could have
changed a great deal about my college
football playing experience.*

I attended and graduated from one of the
finest universities in the country. There is no
doubt about that. If you question that, check
every yearly ranking and you will find William
and Mary near the top of any list. My name
will not join the likes of Madison, Monroe,
Jefferson, and Tyler on the walls of the Wren
Building, but I will always be a graduate. No,
they did not rank me near the top of my class,
nor did I end up at the bottom. So perhaps
being satisfactory at William and Mary was
worth more than being considered a star at
other colleges and universities. And when
future employers saw William and Mary on
my resume, it opened some eyes. I can say the
same thing about any of my promotions.
Graduating from William and Mary made
decision-makers assume I was intelligent and
competitive. I do not think I proved them

wrong. William and Mary just stood out.

As I already shared with you, academics at W and M never came easily to me. I had to learn how to study and prepare myself for these challenges. Of course, both on the field and in the classroom, I experienced my share of failure. I had to learn to pick myself up off the ground and try again. Nowadays, you hear people refer to this as grit and perseverance. Yes, I think I developed both. And going to a lesser school would not have prepared me in the same way, either athletically or academically.

Some of these things that I speak about I put in the category of mental toughness and self-discipline. When I was tired, I had to learn how to push myself. I had to learn to overcome many degrees of both mental and physical fatigue. I thought I knew how to work hard, but I was just kidding myself. My college experience challenged me in this area. I could not succeed by just going through the motions. I think that happens to many high school "superstars." Everything comes easy for them and that ultimately does more harm than good for the individual.

One must learn that anything that is worthwhile in life will require hard work and individual sacrifice. Many people go through his or her entire life never realizing this. He or she thinks they are "owed" his or her playing time. No one owes you anything. You must earn it.

As a school principal and superintendent, your work life comprises managing multiple priorities. My life at William and Mary, including all my trials and tribulations on the football field and in the classroom, prepared me for this. I learned how to manage time. Time would never manage me. Every day, I came to work with high expectations. I think I managed crises at work better than my peers. I rose to the many challenges that I faced. I believe that going to William and Mary and being forced to compete over my head athletically and academically helped prepare me for these lifetime challenges.

I learned how to focus. I remember my level of focus when I started my journey as a freshman and my level of focus when I graduated. The difference was unbelievable. I learned to appreciate what was important and what I needed to accomplish my tasks that were before me.

I met people from all over the country and from all walks of life. I developed a genuine sense of comradery with many of them. These people were highly driven individuals. There is nothing like a locker room environment. For those that have never experienced it, it is hard to describe. Perhaps that is why I started my career as a coach. I did not want to lose that experience. Throughout my academic career, I could never replicate that feeling. You hear repeatedly, when a player retires, the thing he misses most is the locker room. I get it.

In one breath, I speak of comradery, but I must share that I did not keep up with my teammates or friends. That is all on me. Remember that maturation is a process. One day you do not flip a switch and wake up mature beyond your years. I am still maturing. This is one thing that I would like to do over and implore those that are reading this book is to keep your contacts alive and well. Maintaining friendships is hard work. Only you can make it happen. I think that when I graduated; I did not appreciate what I had. Perhaps I was too busy wallowing in self-pity for whatever reason. I burned my bridges by ignoring them. Do not make my mistake.

Self-pity is the biggest waste of emotion. I spent too much time in that ugly place of self-pity. Get over it and move on.

You may ask, if I was so unhappy, why didn't I transfer? I could not let myself go down that road because if I did, I would have felt like a quitter. I would in my mind have been a failure.

I played for some excellent coaches and played with a great bunch of players. I did not share my full resume with you, but two years after graduation, I reconnected with some of these people halfway across the country in a new job. I know I got that job because of my relationship with these guys. There is a bond developed with the people you have played with or played for.

But like all human connections, you need to

nurture them and I blew it. Maintaining a relationship is hard work. I did not do my share of maintaining any of the friendships that I established in college. I regret this and for those that are reading this book, who are about to step out on his or her own, please do not make this mistake. I let time, distance, and my life get in the way. I find it somewhat ironic that I chose a people-person career and was quite successful, and yet I have such a hard time maintaining any relationship. Go figure.

I also strongly suggest that you live in the moment and enjoy each experience. Sometimes you can get so caught up looking into the past or projecting into the future that you somehow forget about the present. I must share that if you forget about the moment, it will be over quickly. You never get that second chance to feel the pleasure that one specific moment might bring.

Regrets? Yes, I have had a few (sounds like some good song lyrics). One regret is that I would ask no one for help. This failure to ask for help is easy to write off as immaturity, but I still experience great anxiety when I must ask someone for help. This character flaw is something that I guess I will deal with for the rest of my life. Asking for help is not a weakness and you should not perceive it as one.

Finally, as I bring this work to closure, I need to remind everyone that you have a right to be happy. However, before you begin your journey, no matter where or what that journey may be, you must know what will make you happy. And yes, the grass might always seem greener in some other place, but I can predict almost with certainty that is usually not the case.

Going to William and Mary was well worth it. However, the problem for me was I never realized this while I was going through it. One must grow up and we all do this on our own schedule. And sadly, I must share that I have worked with many people and maybe hired my share of those that just will never grow up.

And finally, never forget that you are responsible for your own happiness. No one can provide this for you. Some people may help you and some people will hinder you. Simply put, your happiness is all up to you. Always work hard and maintain that positive attitude, and your pursuit of happiness will probably be easier.

Success in life is always about work ethic and attitude. Find what you are looking for and go grab it. And by the way, attack life with high expectations and always expect excellence. It is the only way to go!

Go Tribe!!!!!

About the Author

Edward Yergalonis served for thirty-eight years in public education, most of those years in administration. Besides being a teacher and a coach, he has served as an assistant principal, principal of a middle school, principal of a high school, an assistant superintendent, and finally retiring as the superintendent of the Rahway Public Schools, in Rahway, New Jersey. He holds degrees from the College of William and Mary and the University of Cincinnati. He has widely presented and is the author of articles mostly focusing on leadership. Yergalonis has served on the National Urban Task Force for the National Association of Secondary School principals and the College Scholarship Service Assembly for the College Board. He currently serves as a mentor to new principals and writes a weekly blog focusing on educational leadership that can be found at www.expectingexcellence.net.

Recent additional publications include, *EduKate Me II A Survival Guide for the First Year Principal: Unspoken Commandments of School Leadership* and *Cleansed: How to Sanitize a School,* a novel published under the pen name of Louis Edwards.